Loss of Life in the Path of the Storm Inland *September 10, 1900* Both Coasts Threatened; Miami,
...tember 4, 1935 Veterans' Camp Wrecked by Storm *September 4, 19...*
September 20, 1938 Storm's Full Fury Hits Long Island *September 22, 1938* Cape Cod Isolated:
...n Canada September 23, 1938 Hurricane Victims Swept into Sea as Tidal Wave Hit Rhode Island
...r July 40, 1947 Plane Scans Storm for "Busting" Test *September 9, 1947* 40 on Plane Ride Storm
...1951 "Hunters" Picture Hurricane Wrath *September 12, 1954* Why Gales Are Gals *September 26,*
...t 21, 1955 Hurricanes of '56 to Be Girls Again *December 24, 1955* Storm Clouds over Weather
... Coast as 200,000 Flee *August 18, 1969* Hurricane Dead Reported at 101 *August 19, 1969* Limited
...s September 2, 1979 Storm Forecast Seen as Primitive Art *September 27, 1985* Daring Hurricane
...ast in Next Two Decades September 25, 1990 Home Clinic: Batten Down the Hatches, Tie Down
...stal Development Could Make Disaster a Way of Life August 30, 1992 After the Storm: A New
...nto Gulf August 18, 1993 In the Hurricane Belt, a New, Wary Respect *August 18, 1993* Historic
...s December 1, 1995 Modest Storm Was a Major TV Event *July 15, 1996* Panic Stations: The Fine
...'98 Flood Toll Estimate Rises Above 1,000 in Central America *November 2, 1998* Hondurans Sift
...oking to Improve Measure of Storm Dangers November 27, 1998 '38 Hurricane Still a Lesson in
... Past *July 24, 2001* Flurry of Satellites to Monitor Earth and Examine Galaxy *December 10, 2002*
...ensity September 18, 2003 Unnatural Weather, Natural Disasters *May 18, 2004* Global Warming
...e August 28, 2005 Powerful Storm Threatens Havoc Along Gulf Coast *August 29, 2005* Hurricane
...lf Residents Learn Who's Really the Boss *August 30, 2005* New Orleans Is Inundated as Two
...ber 18, 2005 Bush Sees Long Recovery for New Orleans: 30,000 Troops in Largest U.S. Relief
...randed in Squalor *September 2, 2005* Forced Evacuation of a Battered New Orleans Begins
...Island Shows How a Hurricane Shifts Natural Processes into Fast Forward *September 20, 2005*
...Storm Grows *September 21, 2005* Evacuees of One Storm Flee Another *September 21, 2005* The
...o Strength Menaces Texas *September 22, 2005* Still Sheltered, Evacuees Take a Longer View
...w Rules September 22, 2005 Miles of Traffic as Texans Heed Order to Leave *September 23, 2005*
...Effect" Pushed Texans into Gridlock *September 24, 2005* Evaluating a What-If Case: New York's
...ve Names: Currents That Turn Storms into Monsters *September 27, 2005* The Response: When
...alth April 18, 2006 After Hard Lessons, a New Game Plan for Hurricane Seasons *March 29, 2006*
...emain May 25, 2006 An Autopsy of Katrina: Four Storms, Not Just One *May 30, 2006* As Hurricane
...ort June 9, 2006 Hurricane Aid Finally Flowing to Homeowners *July 17, 2006* U.S. Report Faults
...n't June 18, 2006 Let a Hurricane Huff and Puff: Coastal Builders Are Finding Eager Buyers
...ut Nowhere to Go July 24, 2006 Climate Experts Warn of More Coastal Building *July 25, 2006*
...Plenty, One of Ruin August 27, 2006 New Orleans's Preparedness Still at Issue *August 28, 2006*

HURRICANE
FORCE

HURRICANE FORCE

In the Path of America's Deadliest Storms

JOSEPH B. TREASTER

KINGFISHER
BOSTON

KINGFISHER

a Houghton Mifflin Company imprint
222 Berkeley Street
Boston, Massachusetts 02116
www.houghtonmifflinbooks.com

First published in 2007
2 4 6 8 10 9 7 5 3 1

Printed in China

1TR/0706/PROSP/PICA(PICA)/130MA/C

The type for this book was set in DIN.
Book design by Nik Keevil, www.keevildesign.co.uk
Edited by Deirdre Langeland
Cover design by Jo Connor
Photo research by Maggie Berkvist

LIBRARY OF CONGRESS CATALOGING-IN-PUBLICATION DATA

TREASTER, JOSEPH B.

HURRICANE FORCE : IN THE PATH OF AMERICA'S KILLER STORMS / JOSEPH B TREASTER.—

1ST ED.   P.   CM.   INCLUDES BIBLIOGRAPHICAL REFERENCES AND INDEX.

ISBN-13: 978-0-7534-6086-3 (ALK. PAPER)

1. HURRICANES—UNITED STATES—JUVENILE LITERATURE. 2. STORMS—UNITED

STATES—JUVENILE LITERATURE. I. TITLE.

QC944.2.T74 2007

551.55'2—DC22

2006022517

A note on the articles: Throughout this book, excerpts from articles that were published in *The New York Times* appear as textboxes. The excerpts have been edited to fit the required format. Source notes to refer the reader to the original articles can be found at the back of the book.

For Barbara, Chloe, and my parents,
who introduced me to hurricanes
and a lot of other, less violent things.

Winds from Hurricane Katrina shred an American flag in downtown New Orleans, August 29, 2005.

CONTENTS

Damaged trees litter Jackson Square in front of St. Louis Cathedral in New Orleans.

ONE

NEW ORLEANS, 2005

It was an awesome storm. Howling gusts tore at the roof of the New Orleans Superdome, peeling away long, narrow strips that sailed out of sight in a loopy trajectory in the wind and rain. Inside, thousands of people were camped on the playing field, the tiers of seats, and in the raw cement corridors. Rain poured in. People were soaked and shivering. But the worst was yet to come.

Hurricane Katrina had roughed up the outskirts of Miami and now it was hammering New Orleans—wrecking the city and setting the stage for massive flooding. Before the storm and the flooding were over, more than 1,800 people would be dead. New Orleans, a huge swath of southern Louisiana, and the entire Mississippi coast would be in ruins. The damage would run to perhaps $135 billion, and Katrina would be remembered as one of the deadliest and costliest hurricanes in history.

From my lookout in the garage at New Orleans City Hall, I watched as a dangling traffic light shot across an intersection like a bullet pass, then swung back on its tether. Nearby, windows shattered and glass sprayed down on the sidewalk like lethal snow. It was 7:00 a.m. on August 29, 2005, and the wind was clocking more than one hundred miles an hour, chewing at office buildings, homes, the Superdome—everything in the city.

As I peered out through the gaps in a latticed brick wall, a big sheet of twisted tin came skidding and tumbling at me, then spun away like an out-of-control toboggan. Somewhere, there was the crash of glass—more windows were breaking. The metal garage door clanged against wrought-iron gates. It buckled like a prizefighter taking a punch to the midsection, shuddered, then straightened out, only to be banged and buckled again.

Outside, cars lined the sidewalks, parked nose to tail as they would have been on any ordinary day in the center of one of America's great cities, a city of jazz and Creole culture and old-fashioned houses with gingerbread and wrought-iron trim.

But on this day, New Orleans was not itself. The city and its people—at least those who had not fled—were tucked in, off the streets. The music had stopped. Clubs and restaurants were closed. Even the police were hunkered down. Water was rising in the downtown streets. Soon it would cover the tires of the parked cars; in some places, it would rise above their hoods. The wind and the rain owned the city. The storm had taken over.

That is what hurricanes do. They stop the world—your world, when they choose to come your way. They are among the most powerful, most mysterious forces on earth, and they have been terrorizing people along the shores of the Atlantic Ocean, the Caribbean Sea, and the Gulf of Mexico for centuries.

The Mayan Indians in Central America, whose civilization faded long before the first Europeans arrived in the fifteenth century, provided the word *Hurakan*—probably the earliest version of the name we use today for these monstrous storms. Hurakan was the Mayan god of the big wind, and his image was chiseled into the walls of Mayan temples. In the Caribbean, the Taino, Carib, and Arawak Indians cowered before an evil god they called *Hurican*. Early explorers in the new world picked up the native names. In

Cyclones, typhoons, and hurricanes are the same kind of violent tropical storm, a spiral of high winds and heavy rain, but the names differ depending on where the storms occur.

The United States is often hit by hurricanes, the name used to describe a storm with winds blowing faster than seventy-four miles an hour in the North Atlantic, eastern North Pacific, or western South Pacific. The same storm would be called a typhoon in the China Sea and western North Pacific.

Cyclone is used for such a storm in the Arabian Sea, the Bay of Bengal, and the South Indian Ocean.

Because of the spinning of the earth, a tropical storm's spiral is counterclockwise above the equator and clockwise below the equator.

Spanish, the word became *huracan*. In English it was *hurricane*.

Christopher Columbus got tangled up in hurricanes in the Caribbean in 1493 and 1494 and, according to his journal, was determined not to run into one again. "Nothing but the service of God and the extension of the monarchy would induce me to expose myself to such dangers," he wrote.

The ancients personalized the hurricane, believing that it was bearing down on them as punishment for something they had done—or not done. These days, there is more science and less superstition. Yet we humanize hurricanes with familiar names, and the big ones become folkloric characters, their rampages woven into the histories of American towns and cities.

We may tell ourselves that hurricanes most certainly do not have minds of their own. But sometimes I've seriously wondered as I've driven through shattered neighborhoods and seen the way the wind has danced and teased and destroyed.

I grew up in south Florida and I've been through more than a dozen

Canal Street in New Orleans at the height of Katrina, which caused $135 billion in damage.

hurricanes. I survived the first when I was six years old. My mother and my younger brother and I had taken shelter with some friends in a dairy barn. It was built like just about every other big building in the region, with walls of stacked cement blocks and a roof of corrugated tin panels. It was warm and cozy—we had kerosene lanterns for light, and we stretched out on bales of hay. But the building was not as sturdy as we had thought. As the hurricane lashed the barn, it began to come apart, cement block by cement block. We all pushed to the front of the barn, where the walls were holding. We were terrified.

Abruptly, the wind fell off, and as the relatively calm eye of the hurricane passed over us, the grownups moved us all to a wooden farmhouse. When the wind came up again, the house creaked and the walls flexed. But the house stayed up. We all thought it was surprising that the farmhouse held up better than the barn. But that may have had more to do with the fickle

In 1992, Hurricane Andrew flattened mobile home parks in South Florida, but some buildings remained standing.

nature of hurricanes than with the way the buildings had been constructed.

By the time Hurricane Andrew ripped through south Florida in 1992, I was a newspaper reporter working for *The New York Times*. I rode out the storm in Coral Gables, a suburb of Miami. Afterward I steered my car around downed trees and power lines. Farther south, where Hurricane Andrew had struck with the greatest force, I drove past block after block of almost identical one-story ranch-style houses. And I saw what I've seen many times. Some houses were in ruins, some had lost their roof. But others had barely been touched.

In condo towers, curtains billowed out of shattered windows on one floor, but just above and just below, there was no sign of damage. Mobile home parks had become fields of wreckage. But here and there stood an old model with little damage. Moving across Florida, the wind had nibbled here, passed up a house or two entirely, then delivered a few knockout punches and moved on.

Our culture is filled with references to these monstrous storms—in music,

movies, books, poetry, and paintings. Historians say an Atlantic hurricane inspired Shakespeare's *The Tempest*. In the *Divine Comedy*, Dante wrote of "the infernal hurricane," and Joseph Conrad wrote about the Pacific version of hurricanes in his book *Typhoon*. Artists like Winslow Homer and J.M.W. Turner have captured the power and mystical qualities of hurricanes in paintings. A storm even shared some big scenes with Humphrey Bogart and Edward G. Robinson in the classic movie *Key Largo*. More recently, Carl Hiaasen, the author of *Hoot* and a slew of other Florida novels, used the chaos of Hurricane Andrew as the setting for a novel called *Stormy Weather*.

Hurricanes have always been big stories for television, going back to the early 1960s when Dan Rather first came to the attention of CBS for his audacity in covering a hurricane as it belted the Gulf Coast. Now the storms seem bigger than ever because of vastly improved visual presentations that include multiple maps, satellite photographs, and colorful radar shots of storms on the move.

Easily portable cameras and satellite trucks make it possible for every local television station as well as every network and cable news division to send a reporter, decked out in the latest rain gear, to the nearest beach to capture the sights and sounds of lashing wind and turbulent surf.

The dramatic aspects of a hurricane make it by far the most potent form of weather programming. The storm takes days to build, it can be tracked by sophisticated equipment, and it can be depicted by satellite and radar on television. But its true course can never be predicted with certainty, which creates a long build-up of suspense about where it will strike land.

Steve Haworth, a spokesman for CNN when Hurricane Bertha arrived in 1996, said: "A hurricane is a much bigger event than something like a tornado. A hurricane on the East Coast affects such a huge area. A tornado hits one trailer park, and you have no idea where it's going to touch down.

"A hurricane also affects a lot of people indirectly: all the people all over the country who have family members in the path of the storm. It's no wonder every local station in the East was all over the story. Stations in the Midwest covered it too because of all the people indirectly affected."

The hurricane season begins each year on June 1 and runs through the end of November. The life cycle of the hurricane has become a familiar part of the summer news for Americans: The discovery of a tropical disturbance far off in the Atlantic or perhaps somewhere in the Caribbean; a week or ten days of bulletins from the National Hurricane Center; preparations—from stocking up on flashlight batteries and bottled water to putting up storm shutters; evacuation, the landing of the storm, palm trees flailing, buildings coming apart; then the aftermath: going home, picking up the pieces, rebuilding.

For most people who don't live on the Atlantic or Gulf Coast, hurricane watching is a spectator sport. They know there is little chance they will be involved. Still, they want to know what the hurricane is doing, whom it is hurting. It is like gawking at a pileup on the interstate. It raises the specter of death and the oh-that-could-have-been-me factor. For those in its path, when a hurricane comes blustering ashore, nothing else matters. And it is never forgotten.

Yet for all their fury, hurricanes begin life as fragile weather systems far from the towns and cities where they make their names. The first stirrings often come in the warm waters off the coast of West Africa.

A reporter braves the wind and rain as Hurricane Frances approaches Cocoa Beach, Florida, in September 2004.

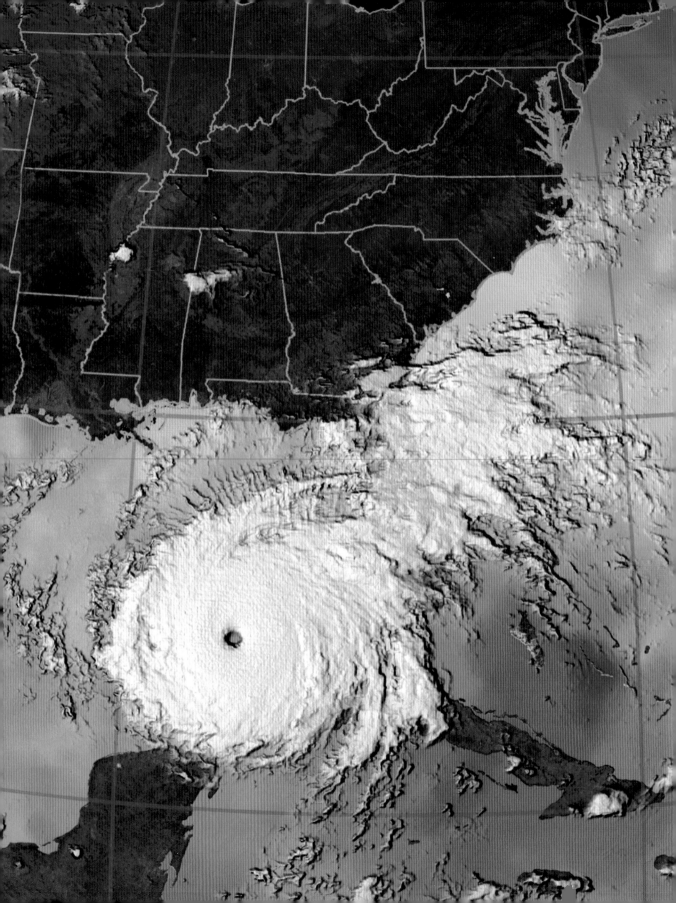

TWO

THE STORM FACTORY

Hurricanes owe a great deal to the dry, hot winds of the Sahara desert. In summer, the desert winds swirl out over the Atlantic from the coast of West Africa, carrying tropical waves (also called easterly waves) that often spawn clusters of thunderstorms stretching hundreds of miles.

At left: A thermal image of the Gulf of Mexico during Hurricane Rita in 2005. Water in areas marked in red, yellow, or orange is warmer than 82 degrees, the minimum temperature needed to sustain a hurricane.

Some of these sprawling patches of turbulent weather grow into hurricanes right there off Africa. Most shift and scatter as they drift westward across the Atlantic on the trade winds and die out quietly. But if conditions are right, some of the clusters of thunderstorms build into hurricanes in the Atlantic east of the Bahamas, in the western Caribbean, or in the Gulf of Mexico—within easy range of the coasts of Mexico and half a dozen southern states.

A poster created by the National Oceanographic and Atmospheric Administration shows the progression of four hurricanes across the Atlantic in 1998.

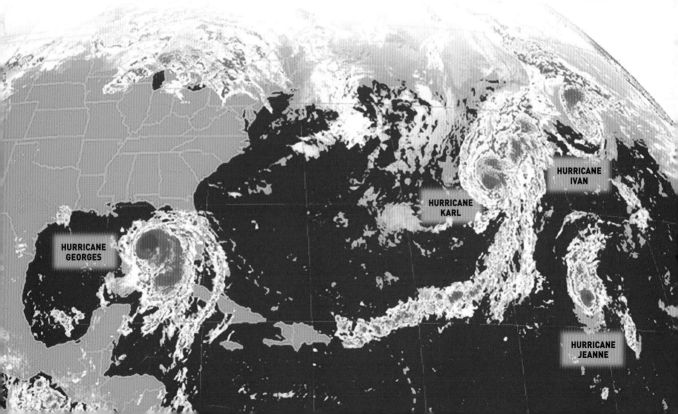

HURRICANE GEORGES

HURRICANE KARL

HURRICANE IVAN

HURRICANE JEANNE

Scientists are still searching for the answers to what causes some tropical waves to blossom into hurricanes and others to drift into oblivion. But it is clear that hurricanes get going in areas of low atmospheric pressure, that they need warm water to fuel their massive engines, and that they depend upon certain favorable wind conditions.

In late August 2005, Kerry Emanuel, a scientist who has spent decades studying how hurricanes reach their peak strength, had "this terrible feeling of dread" when he saw that Hurricane Katrina's track in the Gulf of Mexico would carry it right over a phenomenon known as the loop current.

The current carries water warmed by the sun from the Caribbean Sea around the western horn of Cuba and into the Gulf of Mexico, typically with more than one hundred times the flow of the Amazon River. It gained notoriety after providing the fuel that helped transform Hurricanes Rita and Katrina from tropical storms into a pair of Category 5 monsters in 2005.

Now scientists are using satellites, buoys, and air-dropped probes to study the ability of the current to transform a new hurricane from a ragged pinwheel of rain and highway-speed winds into "a tornado the size of Georgia," as one Weather Channel meteorologist described Hurricane Rita.

Hurricanes feed on the energy in warm water. But while the Gulf of Mexico is often uniformly hot at the surface, that layer is so thin that it offers limited energy to hurricanes, which can stifle themselves as they churn along and draw up cooler waters from below.

But when such a storm passes over the loop current, the water can be 79 degrees to a depth of 300 feet, so that no matter how much a passing hurricane stirs things up, it never exhausts its fuel supply.

The loop current seems to be essential for turning a regional hurricane into a superstorm that reaches the limits of power the atmosphere will allow.

Tropical waves provide a vast area of low pressure. As they move over the ocean, warm, moist air rises and condenses into clouds that often crackle with thunder and lightning. The pressure drops further and surrounding air rushes in. This creates wind, which, because of the rotation of the earth, begins turning counterclockwise. The pressure continues to fall and the swirling warm air alternately absorbs and releases heat and energy that drive the storm ever faster.

Any number of conditions can scatter a gathering storm before it can become a hurricane. Warm, dry air at altitudes of 10,000 to 20,000 feet can choke a storm. Wind shear—a sharp difference in wind speed and direction—can knock the rising air at an angle, destroying the chimney that the storm needs to channel moisture and heat upward. If the layer of warm water at the ocean's surface is not deep enough, the storm will quickly use it up and weaken.

But it is the surviving storms that get our attention. When the wind is spinning in a closed circle at up to 38 miles an hour, it is designated as a tropical depression. At 39 miles an hour it becomes a tropical storm and is given a name. And at 74 miles an hour the storm becomes a hurricane.

At full song, a hurricane is a roaring natural turbine, spinning as fast as 175 miles an hour. The heart of the turbine is a flexing double column of air—like a rumpled sleeve within a rumpled sleeve—rising as much as ten miles from the surface of the sea. The greatest killing power is in the space of perhaps ten to twenty miles between the sleeves, known as the eye wall. The center, or eye, of the storm is usually calm and may be as large as fifty miles across. But powerful and destructive winds often extend hundreds of miles from the center.

Moving slowly over the landscape, hurricanes can batter homes for hours.

The eyewall of Hurricane Katrina, by then a category 5 storm, as it approached the Gulf Coast on August 28, 2005.

Heavy rains cause flooding and tornadoes often develop. In the worst-case scenario, a hurricane moves so slowly that it lingers for days. When Hurricane Mitch crossed Honduras and Nicaragua in 1998, it dropped heavy rains on the area for four days. Eleven thousand people were killed in mudslides and flooding.

Wind bites into angular edges of houses, breaks windows, and lifts off roofs. At the shoreline, the hurricane often pushes toward land a storm surge—a solid, bulldozer-like wall of water—that is even deadlier. Whereas hurricane winds strike with uneven force, a storm surge is a consistent, blunt force that can knock houses off their foundations and pound them to bits. When the storm surge happens at high tide—a phenomenon called storm tide—the effect is even more devastating.

Storm tide was responsible for the destruction in the worst nightmare in

Survivors of the Great Hurricane of 1900 in Galveston, Texas.

American hurricane history, a storm that hit Galveston, Texas, in 1900.

On the morning of September 8, rolling waves began flooding the island—then the largest and most prosperous city in Texas. People could see they had a problem. But instead of evacuating, crowds went down to the beach to watch. There were no warnings of a hurricane and no one suspected one was on its way until high winds began hitting the city in late afternoon.

In the evening, a twenty-foot storm surge covered the island, crushing blocks of homes and businesses. Buildings were swept along in a solid wall of water and debris. The sun rose the next day on a destroyed city. As many as twelve thousand people had been killed in what is still the country's worst natural disaster. Stymied by the scale of death, emergency crews gathered the bodies in piles and burned them. No other storm losses in the United States have even come close to the Galveston disaster.

In 1969, Hurricane Camille shoved a huge storm surge across the beaches of the Mississippi coast and scraped away whole neighborhoods in towns like Waveland and Bay St. Louis, near the Louisiana border. Thirty-six years later, Hurricane Katrina created an even more powerful storm surge that rose as high as thirty feet and mowed down homes in southern Louisiana, drove floodwaters into New Orleans, all but eliminated Waveland, Mississippi, and

In Biloxi, Mississippi, storm surge from Hurricane Camille in August 1969 tossed boats onto land and crushed homes.

crippled Bay St. Louis. Eastward along the Mississippi coast, the Katrina storm surge tossed big commercial fishing boats onto the beach and crushed homes, offices, and waterfront gambling casinos in Gulfport, Pascagoula, and Biloxi.

Because hurricanes depend on warm seawater to keep them going, they lose strength as they move inland. Within two weeks the most determined hurricanes are spent. But in those two weeks a lot can happen, particularly if the storm arrives without warning.

In the worst hurricane disaster on record in the Western Hemisphere, a storm in 1780 swept through several islands in the Caribbean. The islanders had no more than their instincts and memories of how the sea and the skies had behaved before previous storms to warn them that a hurricane was coming. More than twenty thousand were killed.

In the Indian Ocean, hurricanes are known as tropical cyclones. Strikes in the shallow Bay of Bengal and along low-lying coastal areas of Bangladesh have killed hundreds of thousands. In the worst of these disasters, more than 300,000 poor farmers and fishermen died. Most had been sleeping when a cyclone pushed a storm surge ashore before dawn on November 13, 1970. Bangladesh improved its warning system, but in the spring of 1991 another tropical cyclone killed 138,000.

Several times in the 1920s and 1930s the Weather Bureau (later renamed the National Weather Service) fell short in alerting Americans to hurricanes. In 1926, a powerful hurricane swept in on Miami and Miami Beach. Richard Gray, the head of the weather bureau in Miami, first announced the danger by

North Miami Beach after the 1926 hurricane.

hoisting hurricane warning flags at the Federal Building—at 11:30 p.m., as most people slept. The hurricane struck a few hours later. At dawn the wind eased, and for about an hour it was relatively calm as the eye of the hurricane passed over. Thinking the storm was over, people rushed into the streets. Some got in cars and started driving on the causeways linking Miami and Miami Beach across Biscayne Bay.

Gray could do no more than shout warnings to those within earshot: "Seek cover. The storm's not over." Within minutes, the second half of the hurricane struck. Altogether, 243 people were killed.

Two years later, people living in the farm country around Lake Okeechobee, in the middle of Florida, got less than eight hours' notice that they were in the path of a hurricane. Earthen dikes had been built to contain the lake, and like the people in New Orleans in 2005, those around Lake Okeechobee had not expected them to give way. More than 1,800 died, most by drowning.

In 1935, forecasters began tracking a hurricane that they first expected would bypass the southern tip of Florida. Within two days, they

The emergency relief train derailed near Islamorada on the Florida Keys during the Labor Day Hurricane of 1935.

realized the storm was heading for the Florida Keys. Hundreds of World War I veterans were stationed in the Keys, working on a government project that eventually became the Overseas Highway, running from Miami to Key West. A train was sent to evacuate them. Since the highway was not completed yet, the single train track was the only land route from the Keys to the mainland. The train had to back all the way up the track from the mainland to the workers' camp on Islamorada. But the storm was more intense and moving faster than anticipated. The train never made it—it was swept from its tracks by storm surge, leaving the workers stranded. More than 420 died in what came to be known as the Labor Day Hurricane of 1935.

Three years after the disaster in the Florida Keys, another powerful

A trooper searches for bodies in a damaged house in Westhampton, Long Island, in the aftermath of the New England Hurricane of 1938.

hurricane pummeled Long Island, Connecticut, Massachusetts, Rhode Island, and parts of Vermont. The Great New England Hurricane of 1938 killed nearly seven hundred, with high winds and surging seas. Instead of hitting Florida as expected, the storm had curved out to sea to the northeast. Usually, that path leads nowhere for a hurricane. As the storm moves over colder water, it loses strength and soon dissolves.

But the 1938 hurricane ran into unusual wind currents that helped it strengthen and speed farther north than any major hurricane since 1815.

The U.S. Weather Bureau received a radio report from a ship that the storm was off Cape Hatteras, North Carolina. But forecasters disagreed on what the hurricane was doing, and no warnings were ever issued before it ripped through Long Island—forever to be recalled as "the Long Island Express"—and charged up through New England.

Fortunately, advances in technology have made it unlikely that any future hurricanes will arrive without warning. In the 1950s and 1960s computers and satellites were first used to find and track hurricanes. Refinements of these and other technological tools, along with an improved understanding of hurricanes, have greatly improved hurricane forecasts and reduced deaths and injuries.

A microwave antenna, deployed from the back of a C-130 aircraft in 1973 to measure surface winds and wave height.

It looked like a squat drum, weighed 270 pounds, and contained little more than a simple television camera. But the world's first weather satellite, launched into orbit on April 1, 1960, let meteorologists track wide cloud movements for the first time. Known as Tiros (for Television Infrared Observation Satellite), it gave a new dimension to the word *forecast*.

Forty-two inches wide and nineteen inches high, Tiros flew just four hundred miles up and lasted seventy-eight days. But it changed the field of meteorology forever. Before satellites, regular weather observations were available for less than one-fifth of the globe.

Later Tiros satellites carried increasingly advanced instruments that viewed both the visible and invisible forces that shape the weather. By 1965, meteorologists had merged 450 Tiros images to create the first global snapshot of the world's weather.

The next big leap forward occurred on October 16, 1975, with the launching of the first Geostationary Operational Environmental Satellite, or GOES. Some 22,300 miles up, orbiting in sync with the rotating earth below, GOES was able to "stare" at a particular region to maintain a constant vigil.

No weather satellite has ever used more electricity than a hair dryer. But over the decades, these comparatively small instruments have helped forecasters save lives and prevent billions of dollars in property damage.

For millions of people living along the Gulf and Atlantic coasts of the United States, the work of a small team of weather experts in Miami could mean the difference between another hurricane disaster and a safe evacuation in the face of an oncoming storm. It's their job to interpret data from satellites, aircraft, floating weather stations, coastal balloons, and high-speed computers and give the public advance warning when a hurricane barrels toward their shores.

The National Hurricane Center is located on a college campus in Miami.

First image obtained from a GOES satellite, 1975.

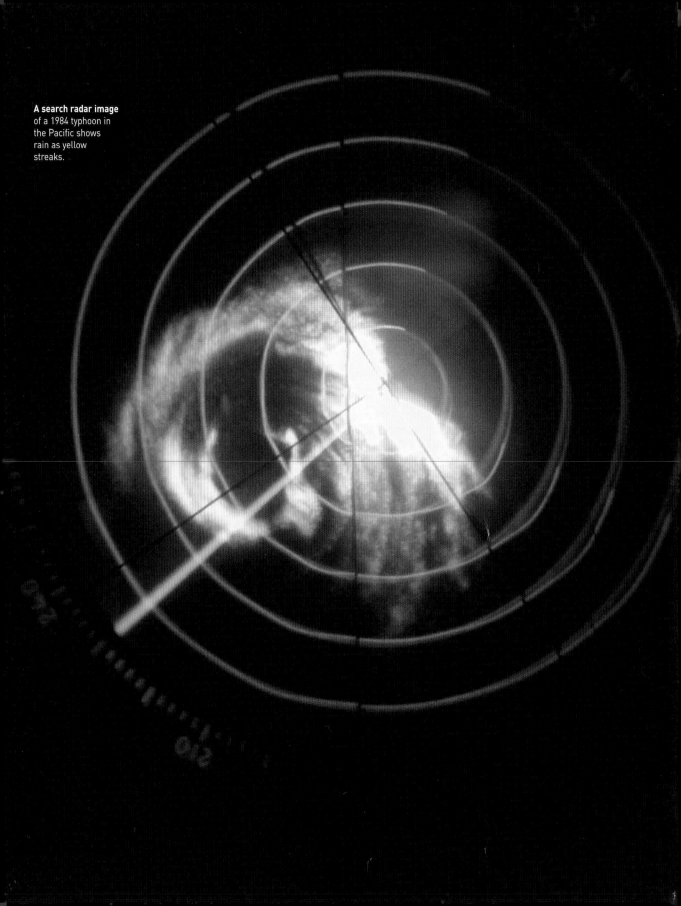

A search radar image of a 1984 typhoon in the Pacific shows rain as yellow streaks.

THREE

HURRICANE HUNTING

I n 1935 the Weather Bureau set up the forerunner of the National Hurricane Center in Jacksonville, Florida. Grady Norton was the first chief of the office, working with just one assistant. Even nineteen years later, when a stroke ended his career, Norton had only a small staff and hurricane science was primitive. He had little data to help him forecast storms and often relied on intuition—sometimes even on prayer.

Norton once told a colleague how he worked through difficult decisions about where and when to issue hurricane warnings. "I usually stroll out of the office onto the roof," Norton said, "put my foot on the parapet ledge, look out over the Everglades, and say a little prayer. By the time I return to the office, the uncertainties are swept away and I know exactly what my decision will be."

Workers in the Weather Bureau Forecast Office in Washington, D.C., in 1926.

Today's weather specialists look to the heavens for guidance also. But their sources are more likely to be satellites orbiting in space and aircraft that resemble flying laboratories.

The first federal agency to report on the weather, beginning in 1870, was called the Division of Telegrams and Reports for the Benefit of Commerce. Twenty years later the weather assignment was shifted to the Department of Agriculture, reflecting the enormous impact that weather can have on crops and livestock. In 1940 the Weather Bureau (which later became the National Weather Service) was formed as a part of the Commerce Department. Since 1970, the National Weather Service has been directly overseen by the National Oceanic and Atmospheric Administration, a unit of the Commerce Department. The National Hurricane Center, a division of the National Weather Service, is charged with the study of hurricanes.

The National Hurricane Center, which houses Max Mayfield's bunker, on the campus of Florida International University.

As important as the work of the National Hurricane Center is to American business, Max Mayfield, who has been director of the Center since just before the start of the hurricane season in 2000, says his focus is on people. "The main thing," he told me, "is the loss of lives."

Mayfield and the other meteorologists and computer experts at the Center see themselves as high-tech lifesavers, devoted to finding, tracking, and measuring hurricanes and, most important, forecasting where they will strike.

Mayfield and his crew of about forty men and women work out of a low, flat concrete bunker on the campus of Florida International University just south of Miami. It has ten-inch-thick poured concrete walls reinforced with steel rods. Its few windows are made of laminated glass as thick as a pack of cards, and it sits on a mound of solid packed gravel and dirt five feet above the highest expected flood levels. On the roof sits a garden of satellite dishes, radio antennas, and wind gauges. The phone and electricity lines enter the building underground so they can't be knocked down in the wind. Three electric power generators and ten days' worth of fuel are always on standby.

Ten meteorologists who specialize in monitoring hurricanes are the storm trackers. In hurricane season they work eight-, nine-, and ten-hour shifts in relays around the clock, seven days a week. For the busiest part of the hurricane season, from August to mid-October, vacations are out of the question.

The action zone is a big open bay in the center of the bunker. It has two facing desks in the middle of the floor and an arc of about a dozen big-screen

Mayfield with members of his staff as they chart the course of Alberto, the first hurricane of the 2006 season.

computers a few feet behind each desk. The hurricane specialist on duty scoots on a swivel chair between his desk and the computers. When two storms are brewing at the same time, a second hurricane specialist moves into the second tracking station.

The National Hurricane Center gets its first clue that a hurricane is developing from satellites, which constantly scan the Atlantic and the Pacific for potential hurricanes and typhoons. They send pictures and other data to computers at the center and play a major role in storm tracking. "The first thing we do when we come in," said Stacy Stewart, one of the hurricane specialists at the center, "is look at the satellite imagery. It covers large areas, and very quickly we can see the rotation, the motion in the clouds."

In 2002, NASA launched a satellite mission that included a large microwave radar instrument, called SeaWinds.

SeaWinds was the third in a series of instruments in space that sense ripples caused by winds near the ocean surface, which scientists use to calculate wind speed and direction.

Winds play a major role in weather and climate, affecting the exchange of moisture, heat, and greenhouse gases between the atmosphere and the oceans. Every two days the SeaWinds instrument maps wind speed and direction across 90 percent of the earth's ice-free oceans.

Up to fifteen times a day, SeaWinds beams data for use by the National Oceanic and Atmospheric Administration and other agencies in improving forecasting and storm warnings, as well as helping generate ice maps to protect shipping lanes.

The 441-pound instrument makes 400,000 measurements a day by transmitting high-frequency microwave pulses to the ocean surface. They are echoed back to the satellite five hundred miles above.

When I was growing up in south Florida, my dad used to track the course of hurricanes on a map that he clipped out of the newspaper at the beginning of the hurricane season. A voice from the NHC would come on the radio with the latest update on a storm's location, and Dad would mark the intersection of latitude and longitude on his map. With the next update, he would make another mark. Gradually we would have a chain of dots showing the path the storm had carved and just where it was traveling in relation to our home.

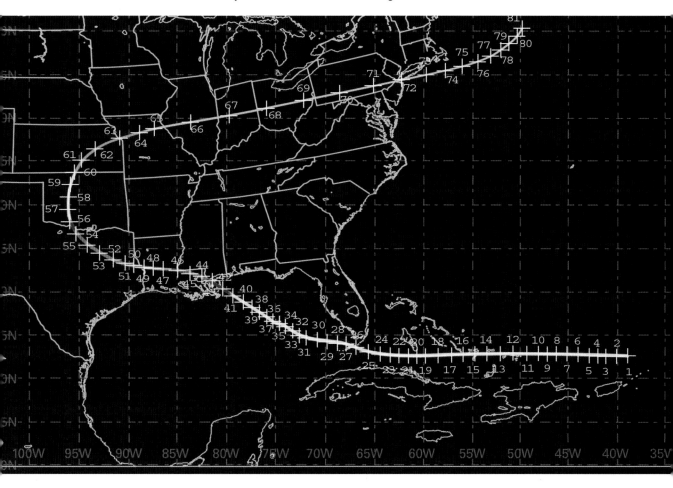

A recreation of the path of the Great Hurricane of 1900 shows the daily plot points that would have appeared on a manual track.

For decades, that manual tracking was the main way in which meteorologists at the hurricane center kept tabs on hurricanes. They still plot storms on an oversize map with colored pencils. But before the hurricane experts touch pencil to paper, the computers have calculated the location of a storm and can offer several courses it might follow.

As a hurricane is developing, satellite images come beaming into the center near Miami every thirty minutes. The pace steps up to every fifteen minutes as the storm approaches the coast. Aircraft capture the shape and density of the storm with radar and infrared cameras. To measure barometric pressure, temperature, and humidity—all keys to understanding the strength and direction of a hurricane—scientists on the planes launch slender canisters stuffed with electronic gear into the storm, and the devices fire off digital readings twice a second as they glide down under little parachutes to the churning sea.

The first time anyone tried to fly into a hurricane, it was on a lark. It happened in 1943 in the middle of World War II. Colonel Joseph B. Duckworth was running an Army Air Corps school in Bryan, Texas. A hurricane was moving up the Gulf of Mexico, and plans were being made to fly the extremely stable but rather graceless single-engine AT-6 training aircraft to safety.

Some swaggering British student pilots who had flown combat missions over Europe started kidding Duckworth about how fragile the American-made planes were. Like any self-respecting war pilot, Duckworth saw a challenge. He decided he'd show the wise guys how much stress an AT-6 could take—he'd fly one right into a hurricane. And if he didn't succeed, drinks were on him at the Officers' Club.

Without even trying to get permission, Duckworth lumbered into the sky with Lieutenant Ralph O'Hair in the navigator's seat. They made it through the center of the storm and were back in two hours. Lieutenant William Jones-Burdick, the weather officer at the flight school, learned of the feat and insisted that Duckworth fly back into the storm with him in the back seat.

An AT-6 plane like this was the first to fly into a hurricane.

This time the pilot and navigator took notes. Among the news they brought back was confirmation of a long-held belief that temperatures in the center of a storm were higher than those outside because condensing moist air releases energy and fuels the hurricane. Meteorologists now look for rising temperatures in a hurricane as evidence that it is increasing in strength.

The nation's war needs became the mother of regular scientific flights into hurricanes. Late or inaccurate hurricane forecasts were thought to have caused losses at some coastal petroleum refineries that produced aviation fuel. And there were several instances of American warships being lost in unexpected hurricanes and Pacific typhoons. The military established a program of hurricane flights in early 1944.

At first, the planes went looking for hurricanes. They were called hurricane hunters. Now the satellites find the storms and the planes go in for the details. Flying into the core of a hurricane is still the most effective way to get accurate readings on its temperature, barometric pressure, wind speed, and location. Shifting clouds can block the view of high-altitude satellites and distort their findings—which undermines forecasts.

The flights can be harrowing. These days an Air Force unit at Kessler Air Force Base in Biloxi, Mississippi, handles most hurricane missions. Other flights are carried out by NOAA planes from MacDill Air Force Base in Tampa. The pilots strive to fly on a flat line through the pinwheeling outer bands of wind and rain of a hurricane and, in the most hazardous and most useful part of the mission, through the often five- to ten-mile-thick wheel of the fastest-moving air in the hurricane, the eye wall. Once through the eye wall, they plunge into the calm and brilliant sunlight of the eye itself, which can be up to fifty miles in diameter in weaker storms, much tighter in the

The stadium effect: clouds at the upper edges of the eye flare outward.

most powerful. The eye of a hurricane "is a place of powerful beauty," said Dr. Chris Landsea, a researcher and one of the National Hurricane Center's six hurricane specialists. He has flown into about thirty hurricanes. "Sunshine streams into the windows of the plane from a perfect circle of blue sky," he said. Around its edge, the eye wall is black and thick with raging thunderstorms. Finally, sometimes ten miles high in the sky, the eye flares like the upper tiers of a football stadium. Below the plane, the ocean is thrashing, spitting, and foaming, tossing waves six stories high.

In the heart of the storm just as the eye of Hurricane Gilbert touched land late in 1988, a four-engine Lockheed WP-3D Orion dropped to 1,500 feet above the mountainous swell rolling up the Mexican beach.

Inside, fliers and meteorologists from a team that had been tracking the storm for a week were hurled against their safety belts as they bent to their complex tasks. The computer consoles and electronic instruments that occupy much of the big plane's cabin teetered precariously on their shock-absorbing bases.

In a nine-hour flight from the aircraft's base, savagely shifting winds of 130 miles an hour or more slammed the Orion through a roller-coaster course, flapping and twisting its sturdy wings and turboprop engines.

The big plane flew a criss-cross pattern through the storm, passing through the calm eye at the hurricane's center three times at the low altitude of 5,000 feet. Such "penetrations" are to airborne hurricane trackers what passes of the cape are to bullfighters; they are dangerous, and executing them properly requires the touch of a master aviator.

Flying through the eye is vital to the continuing diagnosis of a hurricane, because the barometric pressure in the eye is the best measure of the hurricane's force; the most dangerous are those in which the eyes have the lowest barometric pressure. Flights over land are even more dangerous, and fly-throughs end when the storm reaches a coastline.

Dr. James McFadden, chief of scheduling and coordinating aircraft operations for NOAA, has flown more than 130 flights into hurricanes.

One time, he barely made it back.

He was aboard a P3 Orion, a four-engine turboprop originally designed for the Navy by Lockheed to hunt submarines. The plane carried a crew of eight airmen and seven scientists. They were on their way to investigate Hurricane Hugo, which eventually pounded Charleston, South Carolina, in 1989.

They had been briefed to expect a mild, developing storm. What they encountered was a hurricane of great power. They had decided to go in at 1,500 feet above the sea. "You get better measurements the lower you are," McFadden said. But low altitude is also a dangerous place to be—there's very little room to maneuver if anything goes wrong.

As McFadden's plane was shuddering and bouncing halfway through the eye wall at 1,500 feet, heavy with fuel on its first pass, flames burst from the right inboard engine. "The pilot killed the engine and the plane skewed sideways," he said. "We were being tossed around pretty severely. The crew was fighting to gain control. We finally recovered at 790 feet."

Members of the crew of a hurricane hunting aircraft in the 1980s.

The plane leveled off in the quiet of the eye, circled to dump fuel, then slowly climbed to 10,000 feet, where there was less turbulance. Then it lurched through the eye wall and headed for home. That was the last time NOAA crews made an initial foray into a hurricane at low level. The air force still routinely flies into developing storms at 1,500 feet, but for full-fledged hurricanes they operate at about 10,000 feet, which is also better for the data canisters that the scientists shoot into the storm, because they can capture a wider range of atmospheric samples as they fall.

Six planes have disappeared flying into hurricanes and typhoons at low level, the aircraft and their crews never found. But it has been thirty years since the last plane crashed, and hundreds of other flights have been flown into hurricanes and typhoons without losses. One near miss in 1964 in Hurricane Cleo, one hundred miles south-southwest of Puerto Rico, gives a sense of what hurricane winds can do to an aircraft. Going into the eye wall, a four-engine Constellation hit an updraft that ripped off a wing-tip fuel tank and part of the left wing. Then a downdraft tore off the right wing-tip tank and part of that wing. The pilot managed to fly the crippled plane back to base, but some crewmen were badly injured.

The WP-3D Orion and Gulfstream IV, modified corporate jets currently in use as hurricane hunters.

For nearly ten years NOAA has been using a modified corporate jet, a sleek, compact Gulfstream IV, to cruise the outer winds of storms at about 45,000 feet, looking for the jet stream and other wind currents that grow out of high and low pressure areas and could steer hurricanes. "Think of a hurricane like a leaf in a stream being pushed around by everything around it," Dr. Landsea, the hurricane specialist, said. The little jet aircraft and its instruments enable scientists to see the forces jostling a hurricane. With the use of the plane, they say, their forecasts have improved by at least 25 percent.

But the days of manned flights into hurricanes may be numbered. In the fall of 2005, the federal government sent the first remote-controlled aircraft into Tropical Storm Ophelia. It was a tiny drone that could carry only a fraction of the gear of the standard hurricane planes, and it lacked the power to fly against the wind of a hurricane. But it was able to gather the basic data. Bigger drones and miniaturized instruments are likely in the future, some experts say, and in time, human crews may be relieved of the dangerous and exciting job of exploring hurricanes.

Drones like the Predator Unmanned Aerial Vehicle (UAV) may take the place of manned flights into hurricanes.

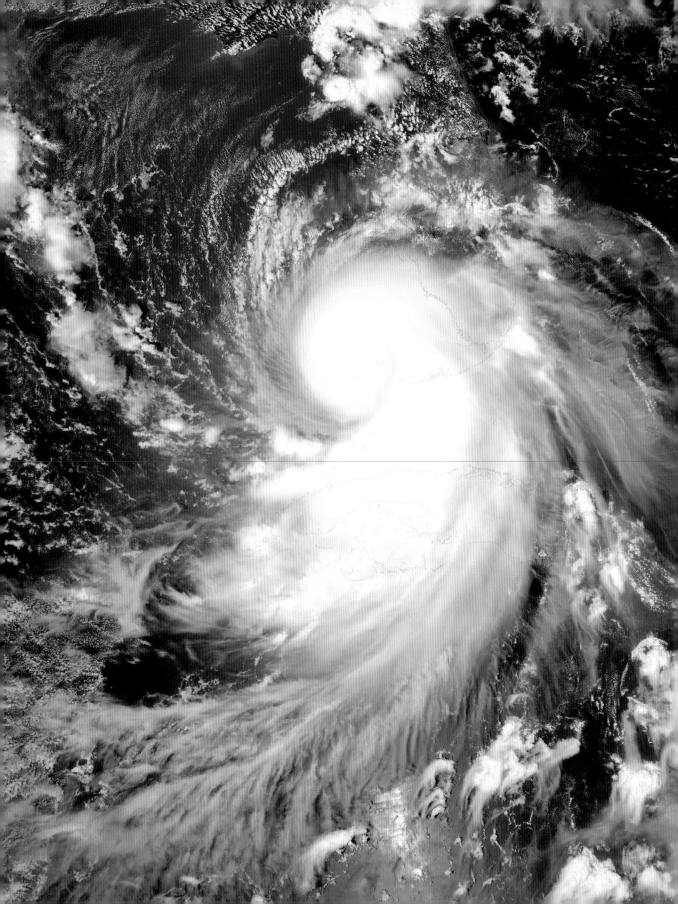

FOUR

DEFINING THE DANGER

When instrument readings indicate that a weather system has reached the intensity of a tropical storm, it is given a name. Forecasters have been naming storms since at least the early 1950s.

The idea of naming hurricanes may have come from a 1941 novel called *Storm*, by George R. Stewart. Or it may be that some meteorologists were already privately naming hurricanes and the novelist got the idea from them. In any case, in 1950 the weather officials labeled the first storm of that hurricane season Hurricane Able. Then came Baker, Charlie, Dog, and other names from the international phonetic code of that era. In 1953 weather officials began naming hurricanes after women, and in 1979 men's names came into use as well. The World Meteorological Organization, an agency of the United Nations, draws up lists of names for hurricanes, running through the alphabet and alternating between male and female names but omitting names that begin with the letter q, u, x, y, or z. Somewhat like the jerseys of great athletes, the names of hurricanes that achieve notoriety—like Camille in 1969, Hugo in 1989, Andrew in 1992, and Katrina in 2005—are retired for posterity. In most years, twenty-one names are enough to cover all the tropical storms that develop. But in years when there are more than twenty-one named storms, the authorities turn to the Greek alphabet, and the twenty-second storm becomes Tropical Storm or Hurricane Alpha.

The names make it easier to keep track—especially when several storms are brewing at the same time. In 1928 two hurricanes headed for Florida a few days apart. The first faded away, but the second gained strength and killed 2,800 people around Lake Okeechobee in the middle of the state. Some people mistakenly thought there was only one storm and failed to take precautions until the second hurricane was almost on top of them.

A satellite photograph shows Hurricane Katrina crossing Florida on August 27, 2005.

You might think that tracking a hurricane would be pretty straightforward. After all, it's a huge concoction of wind and rain and dark clouds and lightning that often sprawls over several hundred miles. But for all their gadgetry and experience and devotion to saving lives, scientists still cannot supply the most fundamental and useful information on a hurricane: exactly where it will strike and how much force it will be packing. Storms no longer seem to spring up out of nowhere. But they regularly surprise the experts by suddenly changing direction or, as if tapped by some wizard's wand, changing in a matter of a few hours from a mild kitten of a wind into a wild, raging monster, hungry for homes and people.

As recently as three decades ago, hurricane forecasters felt lucky if, three days out, they were able to predict within 450 miles the location where a hurricane would hit the shore, or make landfall. That is a huge sweep of geography, roughly the distance from Miami, Florida, to Savannah, Georgia, encompassing nearly the entire east coast of Florida and then some.

By the early years of the twenty-first century the forecasters' margin of error had been reduced by about 50 percent. And over a shorter period, twenty-four hours, they were often able to estimate within a

Max Mayfield talks to officials on a phone while examining satellite imagery of Hurricane Charley in 2004.

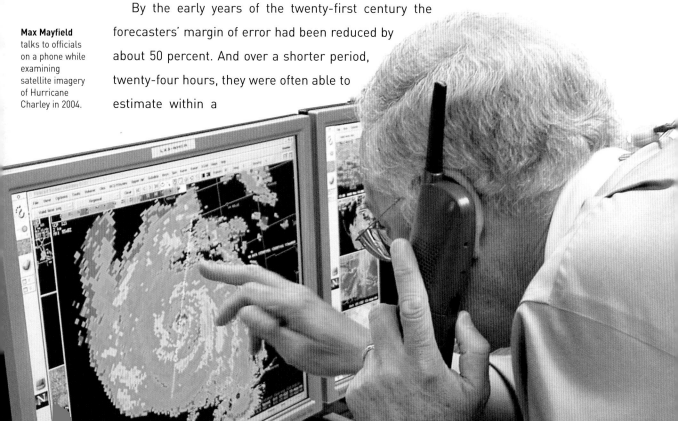

hundred miles where the center of a storm would hit. But that is still a pretty good-size swath—from south of Miami, for example, to north of West Palm Beach. But it is reasonable for measuring hurricanes, because damaging winds routinely extend over even greater distances.

In the summer of 2004, Max Mayfield and the others at the National Hurricane Center got a surprise on the direction of Hurricane Charley. As late as the morning of August 13, they had been predicting that the hurricane would come ashore in the vicinity of Tampa, the largest city on the Gulf Coast of Florida. Tens of thousands of residents fled. But the hurricane veered inland sooner than expected and by late afternoon was splintering the towns of Port Charlotte and Punta Gorda. Tampa, eighty miles to the north, got no more than some rain and gusting wind.

Mayfield, who regularly cautions that forecasters are not capable of pinpoint accuracy, had issued a hurricane warning for Port Charlotte, Punta Gorda, and other coastal towns and cities, including Tampa, well before Hurricane Charley came across the beaches. The storm came ashore within what the hurricane center considers its margin of error. But not everyone understood that. Some residents of Punta Gorda told me that because they believed the hurricane was headed for Tampa, they had decided not to evacuate. When they realized they were in the crosshairs of the storm, they said, it was too late to make a run for it.

The forecasters also missed on their prediction of Hurricane Katrina's path in Florida. They expected it to shoot straight across the state from the Atlantic to the Gulf Coast. Instead, it moved inland for a few miles, then went south

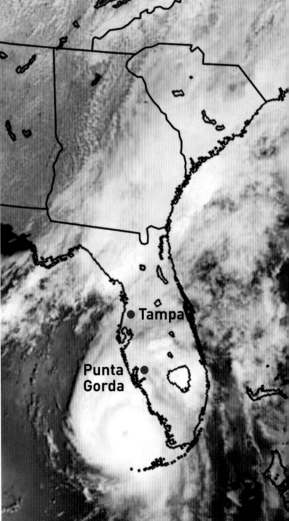

The Hurricane Center predicted Charley would hit land at Tampa, Florida, in 2004. Instead it turned inland further south, hitting Punta Gorda.

Tampa

Punta Gorda

on a diagonal past the outskirts of Miami and into the Gulf of Mexico. The storm's course took it through less populated areas than anticipated and no one complained.

Advances in technology over the past fifteen years have made predicting the path of a hurricane far more accurate, but forecasters have been less successful in predicting the strength of hurricanes, a characteristic almost as important as the storms' routes in determining their potential for destruction.

Better prediction of intensity is important because an increase in winds of just twenty or thirty miles per hour can vastly increase the scale of damage and threat to life.

Perhaps the biggest gap in understanding, experts say, concerns the interface between a hurricane and the ocean waters beneath. The warmth in tropical waters fuels a storm as energy is transferred from ocean to air through evaporation. But once a hurricane has formed, friction between the air and water can weaken it.

In a strong storm, the wind rips at the ocean so violently that it becomes impossible to neatly define the boundary between water and wind, says Dr. Kerry A. Emanuel, a researcher at the Massachusetts Institute of Technology.

"You go from bubble-filled water to spray-filled air," Dr. Emanuel says. "You can't point your finger and say, 'There is the surface of the ocean.'"

Designers of computer models that simulate hurricanes cannot yet replicate that blinding brew of conditions.

A churning hurricane can pull cold ocean water to the surface, rapidly stifling its own growth. But there is a lack of data on temperatures beneath the surface of waters ahead of an approaching hurricane. Satellites constantly monitor surface temperatures of the sea but cannot determine temperatures of deeper layers.

Calculating changes in a storm's intensity is also tricky business. "It's the one thing we can't predict with any degree of confidence at all," said Robert H. Simpson, the director of the National Hurricane Center in the late 1960s and early 1970s, and a person who is widely regarded as one of the most influential figures in hurricane research and forecasting.

Until 1972, the National Hurricane Center had a difficult time advising people about just what to expect from a given storm. The forecasters could say how big a hurricane was, how fast it was moving, and the speed of its winds. But experts had no universal system that could explain the likely impact of the hurricane. The Red Cross would call the National Hurricane Center, recalled Simpson, and ask what preparations they should make and how bad it was going to be. He would get the same call from the Salvation Army. He could help one or two relief agencies. But he could not spare the time to deal with every agency, every town and city that called. He was also handicapped by limited knowledge of local conditions, and began to think it would be useful to have a tool that emergency workers could apply wherever they were.

Finally, Simpson came up with a solution. He knew that his friend Herbert S. Saffir, an engineer who had helped write the building code for what is now Miami-Dade County, had worked out measurements for the United Nations on the effects of high winds on buildings all over the world. Simpson suggested that they combine Saffir's work on hurricane winds with his own research on storm surge. The result was the Saffir-Simpson Hurricane Potential Damage Scale.

The guide, often referred to in news reports as the Saffir-Simpson Scale, ranks hurricanes in categories from 1 to 5.

Category 1: winds of 74 to 95 mph, storm surge of four to five feet; overall expected damage: minimal.

Category 2: winds of 96 to 110 mph, storm surge of six to eight feet; overall expected damage: moderate.

Category 3: winds of 111 to 130 mph, storm surge of nine to twelve feet; overall expected damage: extensive.

Category 4: winds of 131 to 155 mph, storm surge of thirteen to eighteen feet; overall expected damage: extreme.

Category 5: winds greater than 155 mph, storm surge greater than eighteen feet; overall expected damage: catastrophic.

Simpson wanted the scale restricted for use only by emergency officials. He was concerned that the general public might misinterpret the categories. And he may have been right. In 2005, when Hurricane Katrina moved toward south Florida as a category 1 storm, many people shrugged. They would stock up on supplies and put up their shutters if a category 4 or 5 storm was on the way, maybe even a category 3. But a category 1? Forget about it.

Katrina hit just north of Miami one evening in August and left behind a huge mess. Trees and shrubs were torn up; flimsy signs were blown away. Not many homes were destroyed or roofs torn off. But the storm brought a lot of rain, and large sections of Miami and its southern suburbs were flooded. Fourteen people died. A million homes were left without electricity. In Miami, reporting on the storm, I watched an official of one of the suburbs in a television interview, standing in water almost up to her knees on a street lined with waterlogged homes. She had figured a category 1 hurricane would not amount to much. "We never expected this," she said.

Residents of Fort Lauderdale are caught off-guard by Hurricane Katrina, which had at first been described as a category 1 storm.

Bruce Rubin, a public relations executive in Miami and New York, has been through several hurricanes, including the 1992 storm they all talk about in Miami, Hurricane Andrew, which forever changed the landscape. He wonders whether the Saffir-Simpson Scale ought to be modified to eliminate the reference to damage as minimal and to stress that there are no harmless hurricanes.

"It's become almost counterproductive," Rubin said of the scale. "People see a category 1 storm predicted and they think it's nothing."

The lack of caution in the face of lower-scale storms concerns Max Mayfield, too. "No question about it," he told me. "Even with the media, it's almost, if it's not a major hurricane they don't pay much attention; they don't give it the attention it's due."

The situation can be even worse if the force of the hurricane changes as it approaches the coast. The closer to shore a hurricane intensifies, the more dangerous the situation. "My greatest fear is having people go to bed prepared for, say, a category 1 hurricane and wake up to a major hurricane like Katrina or Andrew," Mayfield told me.

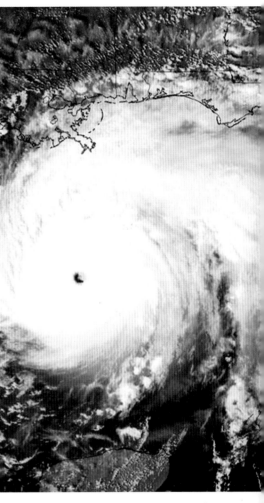

In 2005, Hurricane Rita's strength grew quickly, more than doubling in twenty-four hours.

At one point in 2005, Hurricane Rita was barely at hurricane strength at 74 miles an hour. But its wind speed jumped to 175 miles an hour—20 miles an hour beyond the 155 minimum for a category 5 hurricane—in less than twenty-four hours. Just as abruptly, it faded to a category 3 storm with winds of 111 to 130 miles an hour. The power surge came far at sea, where no one was bothered. But it could have been deadly closer to the coast, because, as Simpson put it, people would not have had "time to consider too much of anything to protect themselves."

Forecasters know that changes in atmospheric pressure and the temperature of the sea can invigorate or sap a hurricane. But there are other influences, Simpson said. "We can't put them all together and add them up to a hard number we can depend on," he added.

When the hurricane specialists at the National Hurricane Center track a storm, they switch on the light in a big red hurricane lamp at the main entrance to their bunker, an old mariner's signal that danger is in the air. And it seems like that light will be glowing more often in the years ahead.

Experts say they are expecting a parade of storms to boil up in the Atlantic and the Caribbean in upcoming summers, with a high probability of devastating strikes along the large stretch of coast from Texas to New England.

Scientists have been debating the reasons for the increase in hurricanes and their intensity. Global warming is the first explanation that comes to mind for many people. But Max Mayfield and others at the Hurricane Center contend that the onslaught is mainly the result of a recurring shift in ocean currents that happens every twenty to thirty years.

The idea of alternating cycles of high and low hurricane activity is fairly new. Two researchers at the National Hurricane Research Center on Virginia Key in Biscayne Bay, on the edge of Miami, published a paper explaining the pattern in 2001. Stanley B. Goldenberg and Christopher W. Landsea said hurricanes increase with a shift in warm ocean currents (called multidecadal oscillation). As these water currents shift closer to the historic paths of hurricanes, storms have access earlier and longer to the warm water they need for fuel. When this shift combines with favorable high-altitude winds, the result is more and stronger hurricanes. The warm currents feed hurricanes, and the high-altitude winds steer them.

Landsea believes global warming may be adding perhaps five miles an hour to the wind speed of hurricanes. But he contended that it was not the main factor in the upturn in major hurricanes.

Researchers believe that the most recent shift occurred around 1995. For the first nine years after 1995, Americans were lucky. There were a lot more hurricanes, but until 2004 no catastrophic ones made it to the United States. Then four big hurricanes hit Florida that year, leaving little of the state undamaged. In 2005, Hurricane Katrina produced new levels of destruction. A few weeks later, Hurricane Rita hit western Louisiana and the Texas coast. Hurricane Dennis had already beat up the Florida Panhandle, and in October, Hurricane Wilma punished the southern part of the state. Only five category 5 hurricanes have been recorded since the federal government began keeping records in the mid-1800s, and three of them—Katrina, Rita, and Wilma—sprang up in 2005.

Global warming is likely to produce a significant increase in the intensity and rainfall of hurricanes later this century, according to the most comprehensive computer analysis done so far.

According to a study done in 2004 using supercomputers at the Commerce Department's Geophysical Fluid Dynamics Laboratory in Princeton, New Jersey, by 2080 seas warmed by the greenhouse effect could cause a typical hurricane to intensify about an extra half step on the Saffir-Simpson Scale. Rainfall up to sixty miles from the core would be nearly 20 percent more intense.

Dr. Kerry Emanuel, a hurricane expert at the Massachusetts Institute of Technology and one of the study's authors, cautioned that it was too soon to know whether hurricanes would form more or less frequently in a warmer world. Even as seas warm, for example, accelerating high-level winds can shred the towering cloud formations of a tropical storm.

But the authors said that even if the number of storms simply stayed the same, the increased intensity would substantially increase their potential for destruction. Experts also said that rising sea levels caused by global warming would lead to more flooding from hurricanes.

That year, so many tropical storms and hurricanes developed in the six months of the hurricane season—from June 1 to November 30—that the National Weather Service ran out of names on the official list of the World Meteorological Organization and moved into the Greek alphabet. On November 29, one day

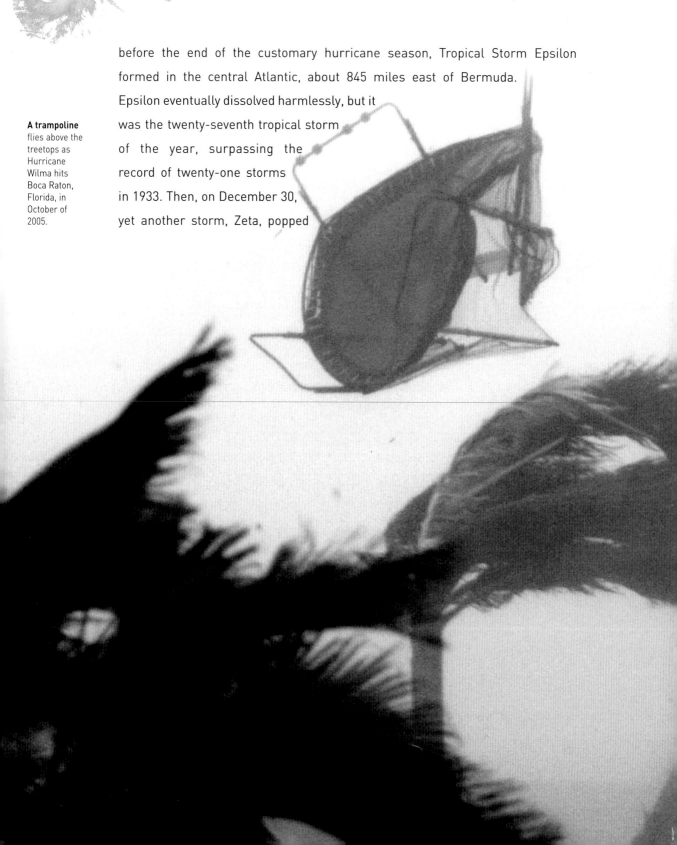

before the end of the customary hurricane season, Tropical Storm Epsilon formed in the central Atlantic, about 845 miles east of Bermuda. Epsilon eventually dissolved harmlessly, but it was the twenty-seventh tropical storm of the year, surpassing the record of twenty-one storms in 1933. Then, on December 30, yet another storm, Zeta, popped

A trampoline flies above the treetops as Hurricane Wilma hits Boca Raton, Florida, in October of 2005.

up in the Atlantic about a thousand miles southwest of the Azores. It was a small storm, "way out in the middle of nowhere," said Todd Miner, a meteorologist at Pennsylvania State University, and it never amounted to much. Nevertheless, Miner said, it was a storm, "and storms are rare this late in the year." Altogether, thirteen storms in 2005 strengthened into hurricanes, topping the previous record of twelve in 1969.

A list of the storms of 2005, photographed at the National Hurricane Center when the season ended on November 29.

	STORM	DATES	PRESSURE MB	WINDS MPH
1	ARLENE	JUN 8 – 13	989	
2	BRET	28 – 29	1002	70
3	CINDY	JUL 3 – 7	991	40
4	DENNIS	4 – 13	930	75
5	EMILY	11 – 21	929	150
6	FRANKLIN	21 – 29	997	155
7	GERT	23 – 25	1005	
8	HARVEY	AUG 2 – 8	994	70
9	IRENE	4 – 18	970	45
10	JOSE	22 – 23	1001	65
11	KATRINA	23 – 30	902	05
12	LEE	28 – 1	1005	50
13	MARIA	SEP 1 – 10	960	175
14	NATE	5 – 10	979	20 40
15	OPHELIA	6 – 17	976	115
16	PHILIPPE	17 – 24	985	90
17	RITA	17 – 26	897	85
18	STAN	1 – 5	979	80
19	TAMMY	5 – 6	1001	175
20	VINCE	9 – 11	987	80
21	WILMA	15 – 25	882	50
22	ALPHA	22 – 24	998	75
23	BETA	26 – 3	960	185
24	GAMMA	4 – 22	1003	50
25	DELTA	23 – 27	980	115
26	EPSILON	28	993	45
27	ZETA			70 80

FIVE

BATTENING DOWN THE HATCHES

For many people, all of the tracking and naming and categorizing of storms boils down to one critical question: Should they stay at home or should they evacuate?

As a storm develops, the National Hurricane Center issues bulletins every few hours. They want to give people plenty of time to board up their homes and businesses, move ships and boats into safe havens, lay in at least three days' worth of basic supplies, and decide whether their house is sturdy enough to protect them or whether they need to move to a safer location. The center provides the best available picture of a storm and the danger it presents. Its official role ends there, and the crucial decision on whether to order an evacuation rests with state and local officials. But Max Mayfield works closely

A sign marks an evacuation route in Florida.

When a storm approaches, the news media throngs the Hurricane Center.

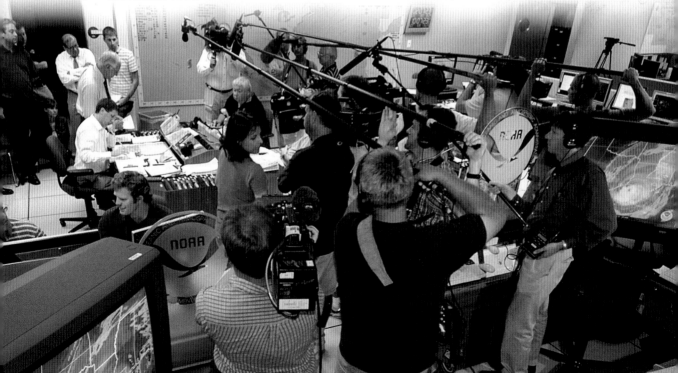

with these others and is probably the most important figure in the evacuation process.

When the winds come, Mayfield becomes the oracle. Television is his tool. He takes to the air when hurricanes get within striking range of the United States and often spends most of the day gazing into the eye a video camera, an animated satellite image of the storm pulsing on an oversize screen at his side. Mayfield delivers his updates in carefully coordinated four-minute segments. Television crews from around the country camp out at the Hurricane Center and take turns interviewing him. Priority goes to the networks and to stations from towns and cities in the path of the storm.

Residents of Virginia Beach board up windows as Hurricane Isabel approaches in September 2003.

Mayfield wears rimless eyeglasses and speaks in a soft voice that carries traces of his early years in Oklahoma. His hair is gray, and there is something kindly about his expression. At first glance, he might bring to mind a minister. He seems reserved, thoughtful, concerned about his people, and determined to be their shepherd when strong winds threaten.

"You have to be calm," he said. "I want to be a calming influence."

Still, violent winds are clearly the issue. And many people base their decision on whether to stay home or evacuate on how threatening a picture they see Mayfield painting—feeling no need to wait for a formal declaration from the governor or local officials.

Ed Rappaport, deputy director of the Hurricane Center, often takes a turn in front of the TV camera. Like Mayfield, he is not particularly chatty. Both men are veteran meteorologists who prefer to stick to the facts. "If the questions are perhaps beginning to stray a little bit from what we perceive to be the most important focus,"

Rappaport told me, "we try to redirect to 'Where is the storm? How strong is it? Who's at risk and where's it going?'"

For Mayfield and Rappaport, television airtime is not glamorous—it is a duty. They are public servants, not rock stars.

Mayfield told me he was not sure he had ever taken the time to think about the image he was trying to project. "The bottom line," he said, "is I want to be sure that people know there's a threat out there."

He feels a personal responsibility. When a storm is about to make landfall, he does not make the thirty-minute drive home. He sleeps on a couch in his office. You hear some of the earnestness of the police officer or the firefighter as Mayfield speaks. "What we're trying to do is save lives," he said. "If we focus on saving lives, everything else seems to fall into place."

Anticipating a storm, a Florida resident stocks up on fuel for his generator.

With a storm approaching, the National Hurricane Center conducts a daily briefing at noon, broadcast by closed-circuit TV to state and county emergency management offices and to the national and regional offices of the Federal Emergency Management Agency (FEMA). As Hurricane Katrina was nearing New Orleans, Mayfield personally briefed President Bush.

Thirty-six hours before hurricane-force winds are expected, the Hurricane Center declares a hurricane watch. This is the time, the center declares, to fill your gas tank, get some emergency supplies, and make sure your first-aid kit is complete. When the storm is twenty-four hours away, the center issues a hurricane warning. At this point, window shutters should be closed, and those planning to evacuate should wait no longer.

There are no firm rules about when to evacuate. But in Florida, which is the most frequent target of hurricanes in the United States, officials routinely advise people to get moving thirty-six to forty-eight hours ahead of the storm. The logic is simple. To minimize traffic jams, people must move in stages.

Get those out of low-lying areas, which are likely to flood, first. Then evacuate the next-closest area and the next, until the residents of the other threatened zones have all been swept out of harm's way.

Emergency operations officials in Florida have learned to plan for hurricanes in much the same way that generals prepare for war. The first stage is battening down the hatches and getting people to safety. When the hurricane strikes, everyone takes cover. After the storm passes, with wreckage everywhere—electric power cut off to homes and gas stations, and grocery stores and other businesses shut—emergency crews, including state workers, volunteers, National Guard soldiers, and Federal Emergency Management Agency employees, move in with food, water, tents, camp trailers, and tarpaulins to serve as temporary roofs. Making all this go relatively smoothly takes planning and stockpiling. As a hurricane approaches Florida, officials move convoys of utility company trucks from other states into staging areas so workers can quickly get in to restore electricity and phone service. Officials learned in 2004 that assembling relief supplies and loaded trucks at a central point out of the hurricane's path can be dangerous. When Hurricane Ivan tore up Pensacola that year, it damaged bridges to the east of the city, blocking emergency workers and supplies. In the summer of 2005, when Hurricane Dennis headed for Pensacola, Florida had supplies and members of the National Guard positioned to move into the city from several directions.

A policeman in New Orleans carries a 5-day-old baby to safety on September 1st, 2005.

In the last days of August in 2005, C. Ray Nagin, the mayor of New Orleans, watched Hurricane Katrina moving westward across the Gulf of Mexico. Early reports indicated that the hurricane would turn to the north and clobber the Florida Panhandle. But by the morning of Saturday, August 27, it was beginning to appear that the storm would zero in on the Mississippi Gulf Coast. New Orleans might be affected, but just how severely was not clear.

The mayor was now facing a classic hurricane dilemma: whether to order an evacuation, and when. Nagin knew as well as anyone the danger of living in New Orleans. Much of the city was below sea level. It depended on levees, or dams, of mud and cement to hold back the waters of Lake Pontchartrain to the north and the Mississippi River to the south. The city often flooded. After a heavy rain, water was routinely pumped out of the streets.

The Gulf Coast has always been vulnerable to coastal storms, but over the years people have made things worse, particularly in Louisiana. Since the eighteenth century people have been trying to dominate the region's landscape by building levees along the Mississippi River and its tributaries.

But, as people learned too late, the landscape of South Louisiana depends on floods: it is made of loose Mississippi River silt, and the ground sinks as this silt settles. Only regular floods of muddy water can replenish the sediment and keep the landscape above water.

Abby Sallenger, a scientist with the United States Geological Survey who has studied the Louisiana landscape for years, sees the problem whenever he makes his regular research trips to the string of sandy barrier islands that line the state's coast.

The islands are the region's first line of defense against hurricane waves and storm surges. Marshes, which can normally absorb storm water, are its second.

But the islands have shrunk significantly in recent decades.

Without the fine sediment that nourishes marshes and the coarser sediment that feeds eroding barrier islands, "the entire delta region is sinking," he said. In effect, he said, it is suffering a rise in sea level of about a centimeter—about a third of an inch—a year, ten times the average rate globally.

There is no way to stop a hurricane storm surge from thundering over the degraded landscape.

The mayor was responsible for protecting the lives and homes of his citizens, yet he was also the guardian of the city's economy and its businesses. An unnecessary evacuation would be frustrating and expensive. It could be especially costly in New Orleans, where tourism was big business, perhaps even more costly during the summer hurricane months than in places like Key West and Miami, which thrive on winter tourism.

In the past, several big storms had spun toward New Orleans, then veered away. Katrina might become just another close call. Once Mayor Nagin sounded the alarm, the hotels would begin emptying out. The French Quarter would fall silent and business losses would zoom.

That Saturday morning, with Katrina's destination still unsettled, the mayor of New Orleans took a half measure. He decided not to order people to leave. Those who wanted to be on the safe side could make the choice themselves: voluntary evacuation. A lot of New Orleans's 450,000 residents left. Many did not.

In the early evening of Saturday, August 27, 2005, Max Mayfield decided to make an unusual phone call. Hurricane Katrina had billowed into a ferocious category 5 storm. Its winds were spinning at 175 miles an hour with gusts even higher, and it appeared to be heading straight for New Orleans. It was a situation that hurricane experts had been dreading. Heavy flooding was almost a certainty. There was no telling how the high wind would treat the city's old wooden houses.

Max Mayfield dialed the governor of Louisiana, Kathleen Babineaux Blanco. After a few minutes, she urged Mayfield to speak with the mayor of New Orleans. After the hurricane, when Congress and others were investigating what went wrong in New Orleans in the response to Katrina, Mayfield told me he could not recall the details of his conversations with the governor and the mayor. "I just wanted to be absolutely sure they understood the gravity of the situation," he said.

For Ray Nagin, the memory of the conversation with Mayfield was vivid. "Basically," Nagin said, "he told me, 'Mr. Mayor, you guys have done a good job of evacuating people. But I will tell you, whatever else you need to do, do it: Issue a mandatory evacuation order, jump up and down. Do whatever you have to. The storm is headed right for you guys.'"

Starting as a tropical depression, Hurricane Katrina first made landfall near Fort Lauderdale, Florida, feeding on the moisture-rich Everglades as it headed west into the Gulf of Mexico. By Saturday, August 27, Katrina's fierce winds and plummeting barometric pressure had served notice of its deadly intent.

Hurricanes draw strength from warm, open water, making the gulf an ideal host. Camille in 1969 packed winds of nearly 190 miles per hour. Recently, as gulf waters have become even warmer, the storms have grown larger and more intense. Katrina would pummel an area the size of Britain—90,000 square miles.

When Hurricane Katrina reached the coastal town of Buras, Louisiana, on Monday, August 29, 2005, there was no mistaking its power. It flattened the town with a storm surge two stories high before moving north toward New Orleans, sixty-three miles away.

Hurricane Katrina crossed Florida and appeared to be heading toward Central America when it changed course and swung north.

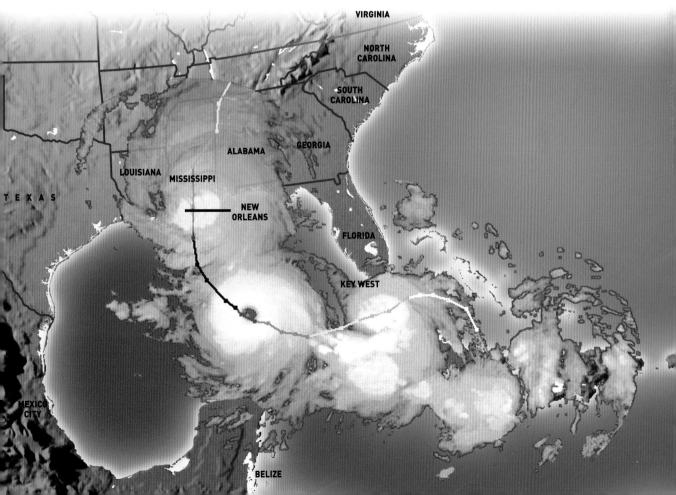

Nagin remembers putting down the phone at about half past seven on the night of August 27.

The next morning, at about five o'clock, the mayor discussed evacuation in a conference call with state officials and the leaders of the parishes surrounding New Orleans. Nagin said he did not go on TV immediately after speaking with Max Mayfield "because any evacuation you do has to be coordinated."

Four and a half hours later, at 9:30 a.m., the mayor and Governor Blanco appeared on TV together to order a mandatory evacuation of New Orleans. Hurricane Katrina was fourteen hours away.

Testifying before Congress several months later, Governor Blanco defended the evacuation. She said 92 percent of the people in the path of the storm were evacuated in less than twenty-four hours. Mayor Nagin estimated that 80 percent of the people of New Orleans got out. But that left close to 100,000 to deal with the storm as best they could.

The term "manadatory evacuation" doesn't mean literally that you have to leave no matter what. But it's a major step up from "voluntary evacuation," which implies some uncertainty about the degree of danger. It means the situation is grave, you could die, and we are telling you to leave.

Mayor Ray C. Nagin went on television to urge evacuation of New Orleans on the morning of August 28, 2005.

In New Orleans, some police officers and firefighters urged people to evacuate. But most were left to do what they thought best.

Eighty-six-year-old Hazel Castanel, who lived in the comfortable Gentilly section of New Orleans, decided to get out on Saturday. But when she went to the bus station downtown at 3:00 p.m., it was already closed. She felt stranded. She eventually caught a ride with an elderly friend and her daughter.

But many people did not leave. Some, like Castanel, had no car. Others just decided there was no need to go. Many suffered dearly.

In Florida, officials make a strenuous effort to get people to leave. But, like other states in hurricane territory, they don't march them out of their houses.

"Law enforcement is legally entitled to take you out of your home," said Booch DeMarchi, a spokesperson for the Emergency Management Agency in Lee County, which includes Fort Myers on the Gulf Coast. "But that is not going to happen. In reality, we're telling people, 'If you're going to defy the mandatory evacuation order, good luck.'"

In neighboring Collier County, which is dominated by the wealthy Florida resort city of Naples, John Torre, a spokesperson for the Emergency Management Department, put it another way: "In essence, you're making a decision to go it alone. We're not going to be making rescue operations in the middle of a storm."

Mayor Nagin and Governor Kathleen Blanco at a briefing with two Air National Guard generals on conditions in the city as Katrina moved inland.

A resident of New Orleans is urged to evacuate after the city is declared uninhabitable following Hurricane Katrina.

In much of Florida, firefighters, police officers, and sheriffs' deputies cruise low-lying neighborhoods, calling out over their loudspeakers, urging people to evacuate. Some communities send officers door-to-door.

Fort Myers, with a population of 50,000, has a public bus system with thirty routes. Pickup points have been marked along these routes for anyone who needs a ride to a hurricane shelter. As Hurricane Wilma was heading toward Fort Myers in 2005, the city also designated several buses to shuttle directly between the hurricane stops and the shelters.

As Wilma approached, Sammy Hamilton, the mayor of Everglades City, a town of about seven hundred people that rises out of the mangroves overlooking the Ten Thousand Islands area of the Gulf of Mexico, sent school buses to take residents to shelters.

In some Florida towns, police officers take an additional step: they require residents who refuse to leave their homes to sign a form letter in which they acknowledge that they have been advised of the impending danger and that no help will be available during the storm. Sometimes the act of signing that statement is enough to convince people that the situation is critical and that they really should leave.

A father and son load up with emergency supplies as Hurricane Frances threatens Hialeah, Florida, in October 2004.

SIX

INTO THE STRIKE ZONE

As Mayor Nagin was sounding the alarm in New Orleans, I was in Gulfport, Mississippi, about eighty miles to the east, interviewing emergency operations officials and talking with people who were securing boats in the marina, boarding up offices downtown, and sandbagging the entrances to one of the big floating gambling casinos on Highway 90 near Biloxi. I was expecting to write the main story on Hurricane Katrina for *The New York Times* from Gulfport.

I had seen Nagin declaring on television that all the major highways of New Orleans had become one-way routes. The police had orders to stop anyone trying to get into the city. Officials in Mississippi had urged residents to get away from the Gulf Coast and had turned nearly all the state's main highways into one-way roads. In Louisiana and Mississippi they call this one-way traffic "contraflow."

On August 28, 2005, a steady stream of one-way traffic flows out of New Orleans.

Despite a mandatory evacuation order, tourists throng the city's French Quarter the day before the storm.

A little past noon I checked in with my editors in New York, and my plans changed abruptly. Alison Mitchell, the *Times* deputy national editor, said it now looked like New Orleans was going to be ground zero, and we had no reporter there. The New Orleans airport had been closed and no one could get in. She seemed to be thinking out loud about what to do. I told her I was about three hours away from New Orleans and though it seemed like an impossible mission I could try to drive in.

"Go," she said.

At about three o'clock I started for New Orleans. It was already late and I was low on gas. One station ran out as I was getting into line. I found another, waited my turn, and filled up. I also bought a couple of empty gas cans—which I was unable to fill—and two flashlights that broke the first time I tried to use them.

For some reason Interstate 10, one of the main highways linking Mississippi and Louisiana, had not been switched to contraflow. I pulled onto the highway and pointed the car west toward New Orleans. A solid line of cars and trucks was crawling out of Louisiana, but my side of the highway was empty except for a handful of vehicles. All of us were cruising at very high speed. I pushed my car to go faster. I didn't want to be driving in the dark if I could help it.

As Katrina arrives, a newspaper headline in Mobile, Alabama, says it all.

In what seemed like a surprisingly short time, I reached the Louisiana border. There were roadblocks everywhere, so I pulled over and walked across the empty highway to talk with a police officer in a patrol car from the town of Slidell, just inside Louisiana. I knew the main roads were blocked, I said, but I was a newspaper reporter and needed to get to New Orleans.

To my amazement, he sketched out a back-road route for me on a scrap of paper. I said if I got in trouble I might need to call him, and he gave me his phone number.

I thought I was on my way. But at the first turn on the officer's map, an angry official in civilian clothes started screaming at me and blocking my way. I smiled, gave him a friendly wave, and turned in the opposite direction.

I came upon a closed convenience store. The people inside tried to shoo me away. I told them I had an emergency, and one of them opened the door a crack. I told him I was heading for New Orleans and needed a map. He said he was out of maps and that he had known right away that I was out of my mind.

Two local guys came out of the convenience store, and I got one of them to tell me a way to get to New Orleans. The other one had a map of Louisiana and New Orleans that was falling apart. I told him I needed that map more than he did. He said he liked his map, then handed it over to me. Now I had some idea of where I was going. But it was getting dark, and the wind was picking up.

I missed a turn and stopped to ask a little caravan of drivers from New Orleans for help. After they stopped laughing about a fool heading to New Orleans, they said they couldn't help. They were as lost as I was.

I drove around awhile and the road I was looking for appeared. It turned out to

A shortage of gas became a major problem for evacuees. This sign was at a station in Meridian, Mississippi.

be a long, lonely two-lane, lined on both sides by fishing shacks and bayou water. It was raining, and the water was already rising and lapping at both sides of the pavement. There was no one out there, not in the houses, not on the road. It would have been a terrible place to be stranded if something went wrong with the car. I decided I should slow down a bit.

Down the road, I had to get up on an overpass paved with limestone bricks. The car did not like the bricks. It went into a big, bodacious slide. I turned the wheels into the slide, as everyone is taught. A white guardrail flashed into my line of sight. The car did not hit it, but whipped into a slide in the opposite direction. Somehow I straightened out, punched the gas, and kept going.

Before long I figured I was in New Orleans, but I was lost again. Now it really was getting dark and there was more rain and wind. I motioned to a man in a pickup truck to roll down his window as we drove along and got him to point me toward the Superdome. It had been turned into a storm shelter

Long lines of people wait outside the Superdome as the storm approaches.

for people who were unable to leave the city, and it was bound to be a center of activity.

His directions were not quite right. But a few minutes later, I was sitting in the rain and looking across the street at a line of several hundred people getting soaked and hoping to take shelter in the sports arena.

My cell phone was still working and I called Alison: "I made it. I'm at the Superdome."

After interviewing people waiting in the rain outside the Superdome and phoning the information to New York, I began thinking about where I would ride out the hurricane. I didn't know a soul in New Orleans, so I dialed the cell phone of Marko Georgiev, a freelance photographer who was there to take pictures for *The Times*.

He was planning to stay at the offices of the *Times-Picayune*, the daily newspaper in New Orleans. That seemed like an ideal spot. The newspaper would have a solid building, I thought, and with all its reporters, editors, photographers, and longtime local connections, it would surely be a center for information that would be helpful as I worked on my reports.

At the *Times-Picayune* I staked out a couch in one of the men's rooms. Marko unrolled his sleeping bag in the photo department. But the more I looked around the *Times-Picayune*, the less I wanted to be there during the hurricane. One wall of the newsroom was glass—that looked dangerous to me. *Times-Picayune* reporters and editors told me the building sat on low ground and that the parking lot would probably flood. Marko and I surely had to find another place to work.

I dialed Captain Marlin DeFillo, the spokesperson for Edwin P. Compass III, then superintendent of police. Minutes later he phoned back with the superintendent on the line. Compass sketched out his plan for dealing with the storm. He had parked patrol cars on high ground around the city and had prepared thirty boats in case rescues were necessary. During the storm he would be working out of the emergency operations center on the ninth floor of City Hall, along with other emergency officials.

I told the superintendent that Katrina might well be a historic event and that I'd like to be close to him to document how he and the other officials handled the situation.

"I could come over right now," I said.

"Okay," he said, "come on over."

Marko and I jumped into our cars and headed out into the empty streets. It was raining hard and the wind was shaking the trees and making the traffic lights sway.

City Hall filled most of a block in the central business district. We took the elevator to the ninth floor. The heads of nearly all the city agencies dealing with the hurricane were there: the Office of Emergency Preparedness, the police department, and the fire department. Coordinators for the Coast Guard and the National Guard and the Federal Emergency Management Agency (FEMA) were there. And Mayor Nagin was in the nearby Hyatt Hotel. It was a perfect place for covering the hurricane.

A man runs for shelter after the roof is blown off his house.

Most of the windows on the ninth floor were covered with steel shutters, a rarity for high-rise buildings. There was a generator that would keep the lights and phones working when the storm knocked out the usual sources of power in the city, and there were plenty of telephone lines and high-speed Internet connections. Earlier in the day, the mayor had warned that the hurricane could cause flooding of up to twenty feet. That was another reason to be in the ninth-floor command post, roughly ninety feet above the street.

Joseph Matthews, a deputy chief in the fire department, was running the operations center.

He saw to it that Marko and I were given an office cubicle. There was no place for us to sleep, but I found some cardboard to stretch out on, and we used jackets and backpacks for pillows. Neither of us slept much.

At about two or three in the morning, powerful winds from Hurricane Katrina began to hit New Orleans. The ten-story building trembled and swayed like a cruise ship in rough seas. I'd been in earthquakes in Manila, Mexico, and the Dominican Republic, and the feeling was similar. I overheard staff members talking about the strength of the building and how much stress it could take, and I wondered if staying there had really been the right decision.

Marko and I tried looking out through cracks in the shutters, but it was too dark outside. Occasionally lightning flashed.

At dawn we went down to the parking garage. From there we could see the Superdome and a handful of office buildings and the Hyatt. We could feel the force of the wind and the driving rain. Yet we were protected behind the garage wall.

Hurricane Katrina makes landfall near the Louisiana/ Mississippi border on August 28, 2005.

At some point in the morning, calls for help starting coming in to the emergency operators. I could hear one side of the conversations.

An entire wall of a five-story condominium in the Algiers section had been sheared off. Somehow none of the dozen or so people in the building were hurt.

But the calls kept coming.

"Residence has collapsed, flooding inside," an operator said as she passed on the information to rescue crews.

A few minutes later: "Female unable to breathe; she is oxygen dependent."

Next: "House on fire."

Then, "Another fire."

A man's voice summed up the early damage: "Three house fires, four building collapses."

NEW ORLEANS ——

The operator's voice again: "Two males on a roof, water rising."

"Water up to windows," she reported after another call.

"People screaming that 'I'm drowning.'"

A man's voice: "People complaining they are trapped in high water."

"Elderly couple in a building," the woman reported. "Roof came off."

It went like that throughout the morning. But all the authorities could do was note the location and urge people to hang on as best they could. "We couldn't send our officers out in the storm," Chief Matthews told me. "We couldn't put them at risk."

In early afternoon, one of the 911 operators broke down. She slumped to the floor, back against a wall, sobbing. One of her sisters had just phoned to say that the operator's niece had been lost in rising waters. Later the officials learned that the niece was alive but trapped in the wreckage of a house, up to her waist in water.

A military officer in camouflage fatigues told the 911 operators to toughen themselves. "Realistically," he said, "we're not going to be able to save everyone."

A Coast Guard helicopter rescue team searches flooded New Orleans neighborhoods for people stranded on rooftops.

A study by *The New York Times* of more than 260 Louisianans who died during Hurricane Katrina or its aftermath found that almost all survived the height of the storm but died in the chaos and flooding that followed.

Of those who failed to heed evacuation orders, many were offered a ride or could have driven themselves out of danger. Most victims were sixty-five or older, but of those below that age, more than a quarter were ill or disabled.

In New Orleans almost three-quarters of the black victims examined by *The Times* and almost half the white victims lived in neighborhoods where the average income was below the city's overall average. Many, if not most, were Louisiana natives, and virtually all were members of the working class— nurses, janitors, barbers, merchant marines.

Because of bodies that washed away or have not yet been found, a full accounting of the dead may not be available for years. But more than 1,800 victims from along the Gulf Coast have been counted, including some who evacuated and whose deaths may later be determined to be unrelated to the storm.

Residents of Orleans parish seek higher ground as the floodwaters rise after the storm.

At about 3:00 p.m. the security guards at City Hall opened the garage gates and Marko and I drove out into the city in his SUV. The sky was the color of pewter and the last gusts of Hurricane Katrina were still shaking the oak trees and flicking fallen power lines like bullwhips. Hardly anyone was on the streets. Once in a while a police cruiser splashed by.

The heart of the city was a mess, but 100-mile-an-hour winds had done surprisingly little damage. No major buildings had collapsed downtown. Some streets were flooded but still passable. The French Quarter, the part of the city that the rest of the world knows best, had fared even better. Bourbon Street was slick with rain but otherwise in pretty good shape. The landmark St. Louis Cathedral, which President George W. Bush would later use as a backdrop for an address to the nation, seemed unscathed.

But those first impressions were deceiving. Not far from the center of New Orleans, the true story of Katrina's wrath was unfolding. The Lower Ninth Ward, one of the poorer districts, was up to its rooftops in water. New Orleans police officers in inflatable rubber boats and flat-bottomed johnboats were rescuing people from flooded homes.

Terry Milton, his fiancée, and half a dozen relatives had just climbed off two of the boats and were walking across the St. Claude drawbridge over a canal that had previously drained into Lake Pontchartrain. Wind and rain from Katrina and tidal surges driven from the Gulf of Mexico by the storm had turned the canal into a path for the floodwaters that had buried Milton's brick and wood house. At least one of the levees that protected the city had been breached. More would fail.

Emergency personnel use johnboats to rescue people who were stranded on rooftops in New Orleans's Lower Ninth Ward.

After the storm came the siege. In the days after Hurricane Katrina, terror from crimes seen and unseen, real and rumored, gripped New Orleans. The fears changed troop deployments, delayed medical evacuations, drove police officers to quit, grounded helicopters. Edwin P. Compass III, the police superintendent, said that tourists—the core of the city's economy—were being robbed and raped on streets that had slid into anarchy.

A month later, a review of the available evidence showed that many, though not all, of the most alarming stories that coursed through the city appeared to be little more than figments of frightened imaginations, the product of chaotic circumstances that included no reliable communications, and perhaps the residue of the longstanding raw relations between some police officers and members of the public.

Beyond doubt, the sense of menace had been ignited by genuine disorder and violence that week. Looting began at the moment the storm passed over New Orleans.

Police officers said shots were fired for at least two nights at a police station on the edge of the French Quarter. The manager of a hotel on Bourbon Street said he saw people running through the streets with guns. At least one person was killed by a gunshot at the convention center, and a second at the Superdome. A police officer was shot in Algiers during a confrontation with a looter.

A full chronicle of the week's crimes, actual and reported, may never be possible because so many basic functions of government ceased early in the week, including most public safety record-keeping. The city's 911 operators left their phones when water began to rise around their building.

What is clear is that the rumor of crime, as much as the reality of the public disorder, often played a powerful role in the emergency response. A team of paramedics was barred from entering Slidell, across Lake Pontchartrain from New Orleans, for nearly ten hours based on a state trooper's report that a mob of armed, marauding people had commandeered boats. It turned out to be two men escaping from their flooded streets, said Farol Champlin, a paramedic with the Acadian Ambulance Company.

Milton and the others seemed in a daze. "I thought I was going to lose my life," he said that evening, wet and shivering and not sure where he was going to sleep.

Over the next few days, other levees gave way and the flooding became the ultimate story of Hurricane Katrina. In New Orleans the floodwaters rose, then fell, then rose again, and finally just stood there like a muddy lake flecked with chimneys and rooftops.

In Mississippi and in parts of Alabama the heaviest damage was also caused by flooding. But in those places the killer was storm surge, and there was nothing gradual about the devastation. Heaving across the shallow Gulf, the hurricane pushed up great walls of salt water, twenty and thirty feet high. The walls of water hit the homes and churches and businesses along the waterfront like a freight train. Some buildings literally exploded. Nothing was left but raw cement foundation slabs.

After the storm, levees along three major canals in New Orleans failed, flooding 80 percent of the city.

Lake Pontchartrain

London Avenue Canal—two levees breached.

17th Street Canal levee breach

Industrial Canal—two levees breached.

New Orleans City Hall

Louisiana Superdome

Mississippi River

Three men in Key West race for shelter from Hurricane Georges in 1998.

SEVEN

RIDING IT OUT

In every hurricane some people decide they'll be better off if they just stay home. Their reasons often seem to make sense: They believe the hurricane won't be that bad, that their house is particularly safe, or that they'll be able to make repairs if the house begins to fall apart. Many people decide that they need to be at home in case looters appear after the storm. Previous storms have veered away, they say. Why shouldn't this one?

Except, perhaps, for small children, who might consider it an adventure, evacuation is a nuisance. People have to drop everything and get moving. It costs money. Some prosperous families hop a plane to some vacation spot for a few days, but most families evacuate by car. They have to buy gas, food, and other supplies. Some set out for the homes of relatives. Others have to spend money on motels and hotels.

Some people say they've saved their homes during hurricanes. But they have done so at very high risk. The owner of a stationery store in Miami told me that he and three other men took turns holding shut the big front door of his house as the wind whipped at it during Hurricane Andrew in 1992. One of his friends cut his foot badly on broken glass. But they all survived, and the man said he figured that without their struggle the wind would have torn off the door and quickly demolished the house. My dad used to tell a story about saving his general store on the edge of the Everglades by climbing up on the roof during the lull as the eye passed over and hammering nails into the corrugated tin sheeting.

But the decision to remain anywhere near the path of a hurricane is almost always wrong. The tradeoff is a few days of extra expenses and some inconvenience versus possible death. Some people clearly do not automatically link hurricanes and death—they think of property damage and general disruption, but that's as far as their thinking goes. Perhaps it's an unconscious calculation of the odds. While a hurricane can affect millions of people, relatively few die.

As Hurricane Charley approached Florida in 2004, Paul Jordan decided to stay with his thirty-eight-foot sailboat, the *Noelani,* at a marina in Fort Myers. He figured he could keep the boat from being beaten to pieces or being swept into the Gulf of Mexico. "If you don't loosen your lines as the tide comes in, the boat can rip up the dock or snap the lines," he told me. The boat was his home, his most valuable possession. He sent his wife and fourteen-year-old son to a shelter and decided to ride out the storm in a bigger and heavier sailboat, the fifty-foot *Black Swan.* But during the storm, several boats offshore broke loose from their anchors and rammed the sailboat across the wooden pier from the *Black Swan.* "I looked out and saw the gentleman behind us screaming," Jordan said. "I couldn't tell what he was yelling. But I could see several boats piled up on his."

Jordan went out into the more than one-hundred-mile-an-hour wind to help drag the stray boats away. The wind was so bad, he never got back to the *Black Swan.* He checked the lines on his boats and ran to take shelter under the eaves of Bonita Bill's dockside restaurant. There he saw half a dozen other boaters clinging to the big wooden pilings that support the patio roof, and found one for

Boats provide little shelter during a hurricane, as shown by the damage to this marina in New Orleans.

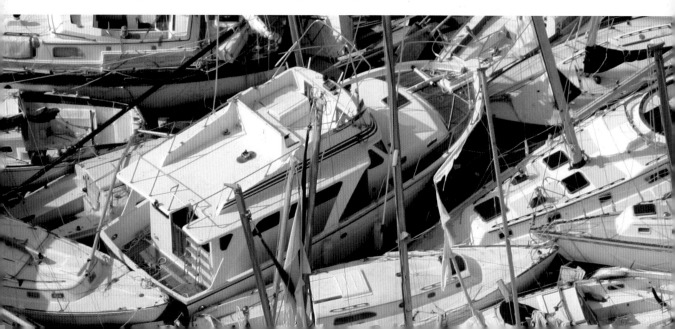

himself. The water rose above their waists. "You could feel things hitting your legs as they floated by," Jordan said, "lawn chairs, pots, a rake, planks from the marina."

While Jordan concentrated on staying alive, both his boats were destroyed. Still, he was luckier than some who insist on staying with their boats. Two people drowned in boats at the Dinner Key Marina in Coconut Grove during Hurricane Katrina, and several died in boats in Hurricane Andrew. They were just a few of the many hurricane victims who have gone down with their ships.

In 2004, Charley made landfall at Punta Gorda, on the west coast of Florida, peeling the roof off a garage and pummeling police cruisers parked at the airport.

Projections of hurricane paths have improved so much that in 2003 the National Hurricane Center lengthened its forecasts from three days to five. The change came after two years of testing showed that five-day forecasts were as accurate as three-day forecasts had been fifteen years earlier.

The newer forecasts create a broad "error cone" of possible tracks, often widening by hundreds of miles beyond the third day. But these predictions can still be of great value.

Unfortunately, many residents of hurricane country do not understand how to interpret the longer forecasts. If you look at only the centerline, the changes in predictions may seem extreme. That line can waver back and forth "in a windshield-wiper effect" from one day to the next.

In September 2004, as the centerline showing the most probable path of Hurricane Ivan wavered over Florida and back into the Gulf of Mexico several times, each new computer run seemed to spawn bursts of panic buying of gasoline and groceries across large portions of the storm-weary state.

At one point, uncertainty was so great that some nursing homes on both the east and the west coasts of Florida were simultaneously preparing to evacuate in opposite directions.

The projected **path** of a storm includes an error cone that widens as the dates move further into the future.

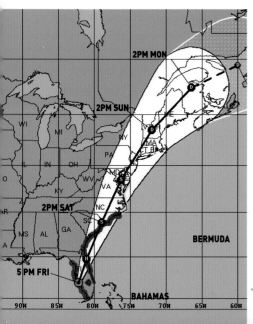

Sometimes people stay behind because of a miscalculation. When Hurricane Charley wrecked the west coast Florida town of Punta Gorda in 2004, time ran out for Christopher and Renee Smith and their three-year-old daughter, Isabella. It had looked certain that the hurricane was heading for Tampa, seventy-eight miles to the north. Then the storm hooked inland at Punta Gorda. "It was too late to evacuate," Christopher said.

Christopher and Renee felt confident about their two-story cypress and pine house. It had survived Florida weather for nearly a hundred years. But as the house shook and windows began to shatter in the wind, they moved into a bathroom, usually the safest place in a house during a hurricane because of the water pipes that run through the walls.

The noise shocked them, a nerve-rattling symphony of howls and shrieks, high wind working on siding and roof shingles, shredding their trees and shrubs. Christopher and Renee thought they could hear the planking shifting and creaking against the nails that held the old house together. Sometimes, the house seemed to levitate and float above its foundation.

"You kind of felt like you were flying," Renee Smith said. "I could see the walls and windowpanes flexing like playing cards. You could hear creaks and moans and things that sounded like popping. One of our windows blew in and my daughter started to scream. I realized this was something we could die in." The house and the Smiths survived, but they are hoping they never find themselves in that situation again.

A phenomenon called hurricane fatigue also keeps people from taking to the road. A wave of hurricane fatigue swept over Florida in 2004, when four hurricanes hit the state. Tens of thousands of homes were destroyed in the storms. But even so, most of Florida's eight million houses and apartments had hardly been touched. Millions of Floridians had evacuated several times and had begun to wonder if it was worth the bother.

Taking a chance: Instead of evacuating as Hurricane Wilma approached in 2005, teens lean into the wind on Naples pier.

Though forecasters have gotten better at predicting the path of a hurricane, they are still far from perfect. So what do forecasters do?

"The cardinal rule is that you can't afford to get people killed because you're underprepared," Jerry Jarrell, then director of the National Hurricane Center, said in 1998. "So you have to overprepare. It's just that simple."

That means erring on the side of caution and issuing hurricane watches for areas where the odds of the storm striking may be low. But this carries a risk of its own. "If you overprepare too much," said Jarrell, "you're going to have a public that doesn't believe you."

As coastal development along the Gulf and the Atlantic has blossomed in the last few decades, expanding populations have made evacuation an increasingly time-consuming and disruptive exercise. But it isn't simply a matter of inconvenience. Estimates have put the cost of evacuating a hurricane-prone stretch of built-up coastline at hundreds of thousands of dollars a mile, or more.

A false alarm, then, is not to be shrugged off; neither is the burden it puts on forecasters. The Hurricane Center errs on the side of safety in two ways when it issues hurricane warnings. First, it expands the area that it expects will actually experience hurricane-force winds. This, he said, is an attempt to issue an honest forecast while at the same time "telling people how to allow for error."

The second way of building in a margin of safety, he said, is to encourage local officials and other disaster managers to make their preparations as if the hurricane will be one category stronger than the forecast specifies.

Sometimes, Jarrell acknowledged, the caution does seem to be excessive in retrospect. He also acknowledged the risk that if this happens too much, people will not accept the forecasts in the future. But the exercise is a tradeoff between that risk and the need for people to respond to the threat of immediate danger. "I guess you hope their memory's not that long," he said.

Even in Key West, an unprotected island in open water at the southernmost point of the United States, residents hesitated to evacuate as Hurricane Wilma was moving toward them in 2005. "Everyone is just a little fed up and tired of running up and down Highway 1," said Shane Le Beet, a diving instructor. "We all just wish this hurricane season would end. It just wears on you after a while."

A cousin of hurricane fatigue that might be called near-miss syndrome influenced many people to stay behind as Hurricane Katrina headed for New Orleans and the Mississippi coast. It had been forty years since a major hurricane had hit the city—Hurricane Betsy in 1965—and thirty-six years since Hurricane Camille, one of the most powerful storms ever to strike the United States, had clobbered the Mississippi coast.

Since those two storms, lots of hurricanes had swung into the Gulf of

Two boys swim through the flooded streets of Baton Rouge, Louisiana, after the storm.

Mexico, but they had turned to the north well before striking New Orleans and the Mississippi coast. Hurricane Ivan had threatened in 2004 before slamming into the Florida Panhandle, and so had Hurricane Dennis just six weeks before Hurricane Katrina struck.

Dionne Richardson saw no need to evacuate New Orleans in August 2005. She ended up being rescued from floodwaters that rose to the second-story veranda of her home in the Lower Ninth Ward. "We left last year, and nothing happened." Katrina, she said, had seemed like another "false alarm."

Three weeks after Hurricane Katrina, another kind of evacuation problem developed as Hurricane Rita began homing in on Texas and western Louisiana. In this case, too many people decided to get moving. At first, Galveston and Houston, the fourth largest city in the country, with a population of 4 million, seemed to be directly in the sights of the hurricane. Chastened by the events in New Orleans, Texas officials began evacuations on a Wednesday for a storm that arrived early Saturday. In Houston, Mayor Bill White urged employers to let workers take off Thursday and Friday and asked the schools to close.

The rush to escape Hurricane Rita caused major traffic jams in Houston in September 2005.

Far more Texans hit the road than officials had expected. After what had happened in New Orleans and on the Mississippi coast, everyone wanted out of Rita's way. In their emergency planning, the Texas officials said, they had expected 800,000 to 1.2 million to evacuate Harris County, which includes Houston. But with Hurricane Rita bearing down on them, an estimated 2.5 million people were in motion. They encountered gridlock and tragedy. Some

cars ran out of gas. By Friday, tens of thousands of cars were stalled on a one-hundred-mile stretch of Interstate 45 out of Houston. Creeping ahead, then halting. Creeping. Halting. Sometimes the pauses were long enough for fathers and sons to jump out of their cars and toss a football back and forth.

The traffic delays were frustrating, and dangerous. With coastal populations growing, the highways can easily become clogged. A mistake in timing can be fatal. "If people are stuck in a gridlock as a major hurricane makes landfall, if there is a storm surge, people will die," Max Mayfield said. "Further inland, trees will be falling down. Cars will be flipping."

As it turned out, the hurricane bypassed Galveston and Houston. The evacuation had been unnecessary. And like most evacuations, it had a price. A bus carrying forty-five nursing home patients exploded. The brakes caught fire and ignited oxygen tanks used to help people breathe. Twenty-three passengers died.

A weary driver stranded in evacuation gridlock on I-45 outside of Houston.

A sign marks the route to the nearest hurricane shelter in Miami Beach, Florida.

EIGHT

Shelter from the Storm

Some people can't just take to the road when hurricane warnings go up. They don't have the money for gas or a hotel room. Some don't have cars. Others are disabled.

They need shelter.

All the states along the Gulf and southern Atlantic coasts set up hurricane shelters. But no one does it better than Florida, which has dealt with more hurricanes than any other state.

Florida, like many other states, uses schools, small auditoriums, churches, and National Guard armories that can hold up to a few hundred people for a day or two, maybe a little more. The Florida shelters are well lighted, air conditioned, and have decent bathrooms. They are stocked with plenty of food and water and, often, with military-style cots. Usually, law enforcement officers make sure everything is orderly; sometimes doctors and nurses are present as well.

In most states, hurricane shelters are efficiently run and comfortable— in sharp contrast to the two main shelters in New Orleans at the time of Katrina, the Superdome and the New Orleans Convention Center. Each filled with more than twenty thousand people, and they became symbols of the disaster.

Evacuating
Hurricane Katrina victims from the New Orleans Convention Center, September 3, 2005.

The Superdome might have been bearable for one night. But it was the wrong idea from the start. It was way too big, with way too many people—very difficult to keep secure and even harder to keep supplied. When New Orleans flooded, airboats and bayou skiffs navigated the flooded streets as if they were rivers. Toxic water rose around the Superdome, and the shelter turned into a disaster area.

Mike Foster, a Superdome worker, was standing in the dome's top deck early on August 29, 2005, when he heard what he thought was a bomb exploding overhead.

Foster looked down: People were scrambling out of their seats. He looked up: The roof's rubber membrane was tearing away and water was pouring in.

Part of the metal deck supporting the roof, fifty feet long and ten feet wide, peeled back like the top of a sardine can. The wind made it sound as if a train were roaring into the stadium.

When the roof tore, about 12,000 people were in the Superdome.

The Superdome, looking like a spaceship downtown, was supposed to be a fortress. Opened in 1975, it had 72,000 seats under a 9.7-acre roof.

But that Monday, as the people displaced by the hurricane tried to sleep, floodwaters from Lake Pontchartrain breached the 17th Street Canal and started lapping at the Superdome walls.

About 25,000 people had crammed into the dome by the third day. In seventy-two hours, the Superdome had become a small city. The stench of garbage, sewage, and mold hung in the stifling heat and humidity.

The National Guard reported six deaths in the Superdome, four by natural causes, one by drug overdose, and one an apparent suicide. Four other bodies were found in the street outside the dome.

The
Superdome
lacked
the facilities
to house
people for
an extended
period.

Food and water began to run short. The air conditioning went out and there was just enough generator power to produce dim light in the passageways. The toilets fouled and people began relieving themselves on the bathroom floors. There was no way to bathe. The heat and the stench, as garbage piled up, were overpowering. Most of the police, National Guard soldiers, and medical aides pulled back to the edges of the Superdome, worried that they would be mobbed.

The convention center was never meant to be a shelter, New Orleans officials said. People spontaneously began moving into it right after Katrina passed through the city. No one was ever put in charge. There was no electricity or air conditioning, and for several days no food or bottled water. Some people collapsed in exhaustion at the squalid shelters, and some died.

Nothing in recent history compares with the shame of the shelters in New Orleans and the suffering endured there. When federal authorities finally stepped in and loaded the storm victims on buses, some were taken to the Astrodome in Houston. It was another big sports arena that was far from ideal as a shelter. But in a matter of hours federal and local officials made the Astrodome safe and hospitable, underscoring just how poorly the leaders in Louisiana had managed.

To start with, Houston officials limited the number of people permitted in the Astrodome. It was well stocked with supplies. Everyone got a cot, and there were more than enough relief workers and security officers.

High school volunteers serve lunch to people seeking shelter from Hurricane Charley at a school in Tampa, Florida, August 2004.

Even in Florida, most hurricane shelters are no-frills places. "We tell people these are not Holiday Inns," said John Torre, the emergency management spokesperson in Collier County on the state's southwest coast. In Lee County, the next county to the north, John D. Wilson, the public safety director, told me, "We open the shelters if you can't find a hotel or a motel or if you can't find friends or relatives to stay with."

For Hurricane Wilma in 2005, the small sugar cane town of Clewiston in south central Florida opened shelters at the high school and the middle school and at the town's John B. Boy Auditorium, a sturdy but plain cement block building with space for about a hundred people.

The hurricane damaged the roofs on the two schools and shook up those who had taken shelter there. But the buildings held up and no one was hurt. After the storm passed, most people went back to their homes. But some had no home to go back to, and they were moved from the schools to the John Boy Auditorium to join a few dozen others who had been made homeless by the storm.

There were no showers at John Boy. But the bathrooms worked. There was plenty of bottled water, and Red Cross workers served hamburgers and ravioli on paper plates.

By the time I got to John Boy, four days after the storm, people were getting edgy. They were tired of being cooped up in a public place with lots of strangers, of having to wait for a turn in the bathroom and having to ask someone every time they wanted a bottle of water.

Melissa Gilkes, twenty-seven years old, was angry. She had gone to the shelter with six children and no extra clothing. She figured she deserved more attention. "The Red Cross is not helping," she said. "Nobody is helping."

You could understand her irritation.

A firefighter in New Orleans rescues an elderly woman from floodwaters. The elderly and disabled are often the most vulnerable in a disaster.

She had been expecting to get back to her routine in a day or so. But the hurricane had destroyed her home and hundreds of others—mostly mobile homes. She and the others at the John Boy Auditorium had nowhere else to go. During the day, many of them went out to pick through the wreckage of their broken homes. Some just went out to stretch a bit. They knew they wouldn't be able to stay at John Boy for long. But they did not know what was coming next, either. John Boy was not like home, but it was not a bad place—nothing like what the victims of Hurricane Katrina endured in the shelters in New Orleans.

The sick and the elderly are in the greatest danger when a hurricane strikes. Florida officials understand that and open what amount to temporary field hospitals where anyone with even minor health problems can take shelter. They are clean, bright, secure, and well staffed with doctors and nurses. They have special medical equipment, generators that ensure electrical power during a storm, and ample food and water.

Florida even sends out vans with medical technicians to pick up the elderly and sick at their homes. At the start of hurricane season, Florida counties, with the support of the state's Department of Health, compile a list of people who need special assistance. As a hurricane is approaching, the counties phone those on the list, then send out vans to take them to the shelters.

Safely sheltered at a local school, an elderly couple plays cards as Hurricane Francis blows over Fort Pierce, Florida.

Two days before Hurricane Wilma hit, I arrived at a special shelter in Fort Myers just as Joseph Giama, a stroke victim, was being lowered from one of the vans in his electric wheelchair. Giama was eighty-seven years old, a retired mechanic and a widower from Lodi, New Jersey. He lived alone in a mobile home.

As his electric wheelchair rolled onto the pavement, he took a moment to look over the Ray V. Pottorf Elementary School, a nearly new structure painted in bright colors with hurricane-proof glass in the windows. He touched a lever and the wheelchair glided soundlessly up a long walkway to the front doors of the school. The doors popped open and several volunteers and county health workers greeted him.

In less than an hour Giama was assigned an aluminum cot in a classroom with about a dozen others. The classroom had its own bathroom, and there were oxygen machines to help people with their breathing.

For a late lunch, Mr. Giama went to the school's big, sunny cafeteria and got a plate of pizza, an apple cobbler, tater tots, and a side of peas and carrots.

Patients inside the Palm Beach county special needs shelter in advance of Hurricane Francis, September 2004.

Steven A. Fettner, the disaster preparedness and response coordinator for Lee County, told me the plan was to take care of about 150 elderly and sick at the school. About 35,000 residents without special health needs would be taken into other Lee County shelters.

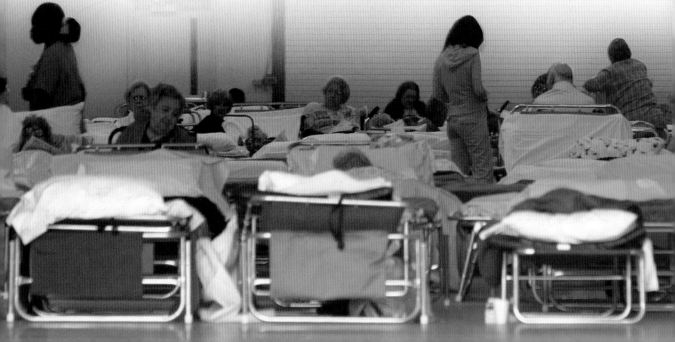

Almost a year after Hurricane Katrina forced them to leave, thousands of elderly evacuees still struggled every day to get by in cities hundreds of miles from their homes in New Orleans. But it is the elderly who wanted most to return, said social service workers, and who had the hardest time doing so.

In the storm's immediate impact, 71 percent of the dead were over the age of sixty, and nearly half were over seventy-five. But the stresses and the vulnerabilities did not end with the storm's passing.

"At no point in your life is it easy to pick up and be displaced, but it's especially tough for senior citizens," said Ginny Goldman, chief organizer in Houston for Acorn, the Association of Community Organizations for Reform Now. "There are lots of evacuee issues that affect everybody, but they seem to affect seniors especially, because they can't bounce back so easily."

"As we found out in Louisiana, when you have a real disaster, it's the elderly who are least capable of taking care of themselves," said Senator Herb Kohl of Wisconsin, who participated in Senate hearings in 2006 on the plight of Hurricane Katrina's elderly.

"They are the most at risk and the most likely to be displaced or to lose their lives," Mr. Kohl said.

As Hurricane Frances was approaching Florida in 2004, the phone rang at the home of Ruth and David Thomas in Boynton Beach. It was the Palm Beach County Health Department. "They said they were coming to get us," Mrs. Thomas said later. The retired couple was taken to a huge, high-ceilinged exhibition hall at the Palm Beach County fairgrounds.

From the outside, the exhibition hall looked like a fortress. It was all thick slabs of concrete. Inside, in a bright, open bay, there were several hundred cots, lined up with military precision, some with wheelchairs and oxygen tanks beside them. It was so well air conditioned that I needed a sweater. A cafeteria line had been set up, and you could get coffee and snacks anytime. Raise your hand and someone would come and check your blood pressure.

After the hurricane, Helen Marcone, who was eighty-four years old and got help with breathing from a little machine next to her bed, was eager to go home. But she knew she could not do that until the electric power was restored, and anyway, she was pretty comfortable. "The treatment here couldn't be nicer," she said.

Storm Surge from Hurricane Katrina destroyed most of the town of Waveland, Mississippi.

NINE

Bracing for the Future

For several decades beginning in the 1940s, weather experts were optimistic that they could take control of hurricanes—literally stop the wind. They tried to break up hurricanes by dropping dry ice, silver iodide, and even dirt into them. They dreamed of coming up with some kind of superstrong film that could cover big patches of the ocean and starve hurricanes of the warm water that sustains them. But nothing worked. And they have given up, at least temporarily, partly out of concern that tampering with a hurricane might drive it into a neighboring country, with terrible political consequences.

It looks like hurricanes are here to stay—and over the next few decades, they are going to be more and more on the minds of Americans as they deal with a new era of violent weather.

The warning flags are up. And for all our technological advances, there is nothing anyone can do to change the situation. Hurricanes are still elusive creatures that scientists do not fully understand, that they admittedly have difficulty measuring and tracking, and that they have no hope of influencing. Indeed, the small community of scientists who concentrate on the study of hurricanes find themselves woefully agreeing with a song from 1974 by pop singer Jimmy Buffett, in which he groans about the impossibility of "trying to reason with hurricane season."

For now, at least, all any of us can do is learn to live with hurricanes, which is a little like learning to live with an eight-hundred-pound gorilla. The hurricane always has the advantage. The hurricane acts, the world reacts.

The financial costs of hurricanes have become staggering, and economists and scientists say the future looks even worse. It is not only that more powerful storms are on the way, but that what used to be vast, lonely stretches of sand dunes and sea grasses have become crowded with homes and offices and resorts. Even with stronger building codes in Florida and a few other states, heavy damage is inevitable.

A look back at the 1926 hurricane that wrecked Miami and Miami Beach tells the story of how an explosion of coastal development has changed the disaster balance sheet. In 1926 the winds tore off roofs of Miami Beach mansions and shattered hotel windows. A storm surge battered buildings and flooded Miami Beach and downtown Miami. The damage ran to $760 million in 2004 dollars.

But Miami Beach and Miami were very different places back then. Pictures of the destruction show wide sections of empty, undeveloped lots that are now filled up. These days, anyone who wants to put up a new building typically has to tear down an older one. Of course, developers have been doing just that to build bigger and more expensive buildings, adding to the potential cost of future hurricanes.

Dr. Roger A. Pielke, Jr., director of the Center for Science and Technology at the University of Colorado, estimates that the same 1926 hurricane following the same track through Miami Beach and Miami today could run up nearly $130 billion in damage. Similarly, damage from a replay of Hurricane Andrew—which stayed well south of downtown Miami in 1992—could cost $50 billion, more than double its original toll, adjusted for inflation. Assuming that development along the coasts keeps on at its current pace, Dr. Pielke says, a single storm in ten to fifteen years may bring losses of $500 billion.

But even in an era of more frequent and powerful storms, Dr. Hugh Willoughby, a hurricane researcher at Florida International University, says it is unlikely we will soon see another storm as destructive as Hurricane Katrina. Still, he adds, it would not be surprising for several major hurricanes to hit the United States every three to five years over the next few decades.

Luxury beachfront condos place more residents, and money, in the path of hurricanes.

Coastal scientists have been saying for years that global warming will threaten coastal areas with higher seas and more powerful storms.

Erosion already threatens 70 percent of the nation's coastline, and is especially severe on the eastern and Gulf coasts. In a report to Congress in 2000, the Federal Emergency Management Agency said that more than a quarter of the houses within five hundred feet of the coast might be lost to the sea by 2060.

According to the Census Bureau, 87 million people, nearly a third of the nation's population, live on or near the Atlantic or Gulf coasts.

"You cannot draw up a worse case scenario for increased property damage, risk to human life, and cost to taxpayers," said Robert S. Young of Western Carolina University, who studies coastal development.

Scientists from the geological survey have been making observations of the coastal landscape, before and after storms, to try to identify characteristics that make areas more or less vulnerable to storm damage.

But plenty of people reject the idea that those who live on the coast are any more at risk than those who live in areas prone to tornadoes, earthquakes, or forest fires, even in an era of increased storms.

Dr. Willoughby and some other hurricane experts take a conservative and somewhat controversial view on evacuation. They say that these days, many people may do best to stay at home during a storm. They recommend that people living directly on the water and those in mobile homes evacuate. But they say a solidly built home will probably withstand a hurricane.

Their counterintuitive approach of not advising everyone in the path of a hurricane to pack up and get out reflects a sense that evacuations themselves can become disasters. Hurricane experts know that evacuations are expensive for individuals and whole economies. And they know that false alarms—because a storm went one way when it was expected to go another— breed the kind of complacency that proved fatal in Hurricane Katrina.

Yet the most persistent fear, for the experts, is that millions of people will start moving too late. Gridlock can then develop on coastal highways and bridges and, while all the cars and vans are stuck in traffic, a hurricane and storm surge can sweep in and kill hundreds. From a strategic point of view, thinning the ranks of evacuees may make sense.

If there is one lesson that can be learned from the devastation caused by Katrina, it is that advance planning, by governments and individuals, can mean the difference between dozens of deaths and thousands. The more than eighteen hundred deaths in Hurricane Katrina were not the result of failures of the country's storm-tracking system. Rather, it was a case of officials failing to respond to the danger of long-anticipated flooding in New Orleans and to the potential for killer storm surges along the Mississippi coast.

That failure of planning had lasting consequences. A year after the storm, New Orleans and much of the Mississippi coast were still in ruins. Empty, broken houses, many still caked with mud, sat dark and silent on block after block in New Orleans. Only about half of New Orleans's pre-Katrina population of 480,000 had returned; about 60 percent of the businesses were still shuttered. Many of those who fled the storm were making new lives in other towns and cities and would never return.

In Mississippi, Governor Haley Barbour bragged that his people were doing much better at patching up and moving on. Indeed, many of the ruined casinos in Biloxi were back in business. But thousands of Mississippians were still living in small trailers provided by the Federal Emergency Management Agency, and by some estimates fewer than 5 percent of the destroyed houses in towns along the coast were being rebuilt.

The town of Waveland was one of the hardest hit. It sits right on the beach, and a lot of its houses and much of its downtown were "slabbed"—wiped down to their concrete

Rubble of a home destoyed by Hurricane Ivan in Cape San Blas, Florida, in September 2004.

In 2006, federal and Louisiana state emergency officials promised a different approach to future hurricane seasons, saying they would no longer use "last resort" shelters like the Superdome to house displaced residents.

Instead, they said, they will put into effect a better system of communication and evacuation to get residents away from the path of a storm.

"Our goal is to create an environment for all of the individuals to leave in the face of a storm rather than stay," said Terry Ebbert, the homeland security advisor for Orleans Parish.

To relocate a large number of people efficiently, Ebbert said, officials are planning an improved public education campaign and are exploring new ways to use buses, trains, airlines, and other evacuation routes.

R. David Paulison, acting director of the Federal Emergency Management Agency, said the new plans were a direct result of lessons learned from the disastrous Gulf Coast hurricanes of 2005.

foundations—by the nearly thirty-foot storm surge. A year later, Leonard Pitts of the *Miami Herald* visited the town. He said he heard some carpenters' hammers tapping. "But mostly, one sees dead and broken trees, vacant lots being reclaimed by nature, white FEMA trailers filled with people waiting and hoping to get their lives back."

Anyone who lives in hurricane country should develop a plan—for good measure, that means almost everyone in Florida and just about anyone living near the coast from Texas to as far north as New England. The idea is to always stay a few steps ahead of a hurricane in order to reduce surprise, damage, and deaths. Every coastal town has a hurricane plan to one degree or another—involving evacuation routes and shelters, emergency supplies, and power outages—and every person or family ought to have one.

Drawing up a plan makes you stop and think. How vulnerable are you? Would you expect to evacuate? Where would you go? Have you got food, water, and other supplies to get you through at least several days without electric power?

Max Mayfield and other experts warn against taking anything for granted, including what forecasters say about when and where a storm will hit and how much power it will be packing. And they add: Don't dwell on what the last hurricane did—especially if the damage was slight—because the chance of a repeat performance is low.

Don't think that you will be able to beat a hurricane. The hurricane has the artillery, the infantry, the armor, and the air force. You may have a hammer and nails. When the hurricane swings right, you swing left. Get out of its way and you may live to have grandchildren.

Personally, after what I've seen of hurricanes, I don't plan to ride out another one in an ordinary house. The house might do just fine. But hurricane winds behave in such peculiar ways that you can't be sure. When winds of more than one hundred miles an hour start ripping at roofs and garage doors, I want to be somewhere else.

There are dozens of ways to get hurt in a hurricane. Sometimes a house is undaunted by the wind. But then a big tree crashes through the roof. Electrical wires are exposed and glass flies. Rising water claims lives and homes.

Hurricanes are fascinating. But above all, they are dangerous. With no way to know exactly what hurricanes will do, the safest strategy is to stay well clear of them. Unless I'm reporting on a storm, you won't find me trying to reason with hurricane season.

Planning ahead: A house in West Palm Beach built to withstand hurricanes.

BUILDING A HURRICANE-PROOF HOUSE

After two years of horrendous hurricanes, with more catastrophic weather expected, developers and contractors along the southern coasts began in 2006 to produce a new generation of houses that were designed to withstand just about anything that nature can throw at them.

Until then, few buyers had been interested in superstrong houses. Those houses usually cost far more and often looked more like ugly ducklings than cozy havens. But many of the new homes proved more appealing. Demand jumped sharply, and insurance companies even offered policies at a discount in coastal areas where they were otherwise cutting back on coverage.

Here's how one developer on the Texas coast is building fortified houses to withstand hurricanes.

House Frame

Every piece of the wood frame is secured using metal straps. The entire structure is bolted to the columns below.

Window Shutters

Wooden shutters provide a first line of defense. Impact-resistant laminated windows, much stronger than regular windows, provide further protection against windblown debris.

Aboveground Columns

Reinforced concrete columns, each more than a foot square, lift the house twenty-six feet above sea level. The mezzanine will sit eighteen feet above sea level, high enough to escape storm flooding.

Grade Beam

Reinforced concrete beams, two feet thick, and a four-inch concrete slab link the underground support columns and distribute the weight of the house equally.

Roof
Secured to the house frame with metal straps for extra strength, each shingle is attached using six-inch nails.

26 ft.

14 in.
diameter

18 in.
diameter

10 ft.

Underground Support Columns
Steel-reinforced concrete support columns, eighteen inches in diameter, are built ten feet into the ground.

Between 1900 and 2005, seventy major Atlantic hurricanes (category 3 or greater) reached the United States. The points on the map below indicate where some of the most notorious major storms first made landfall in North or Central America. Many swept over one or more Caribbean islands on their approach.

1 **Galveston Hurricane of 1900,** category 5.

2 **Atlantic Gulf Hurricane of 1919,** category 3.

3 **Great Miami Hurricane of 1926,** category 4.

4 **San Felipe–Okeechobee Hurricane of 1928,** category 4.

5 **Labor Day Hurricane of 1935,** category 5 in Florida Keys, category 2 on landfall.

6 **New England Hurricane of 1938,** category 3.

7 **Great Atlantic Hurricane of 1944,** category 3.

8 **Carol** (1954), category 3.

9 **Hazel** (1954), category 4.

10 **Edna** (1954), category 3.

11 **Connie** (1955), category 3.

12 **Audrey** (1957), category 4.

13 **Donna** (1960), category 4.

14 **Camille** (1969), category 3

15 **Alicia** (1983), category 3.

16 **Gilbert** (1988), category 5.

17 **Hugo** (1989), category 4.

18 **Andrew** (1992), category 3.

19 **Opal** (1995), category 3.

20 **Iris** (2001), category 4.

21 **Ivan** (2004), category 4.

22 **Charley** (2004), category 4.

23 **Jeanne** (2004), category 4.

24 **Dennis** (2005), category 4.

25 **Katrina** (2005), category 3.

26 **Rita** (2005), category 3.

27 **Wilma** (2005), category 4.

2005: THE BUILDUP

Tuesday, August 23
A tropical depression forms about 200 miles southeast of Nassau in the Bahamas.

Wednesday, August 24
The depression is upgraded to a tropical storm and named Katrina about 75 miles east-southwest of Nassau. Tropical Storm Katrina passes through the Northwestern Bahamas.

Thursday, August 25
Katrina hits Florida, near Miami, as a category 1 storm.

Friday, August 26
Hurricane Katrina crosses Florida and heads into the Gulf of Mexico. Louisiana Governor Kathleen Blanco declares a state of emergency and requests additional forces from the United States government.

Saturday, August 27
Hurricane Katrina gains power as it heads northwest across the Gulf of Mexico. New Orleans Mayor Ray C. Nagin declares a state of emergency and issues a voluntary evacuation order. Four thousand National Guard troops are deployed to prepare for the storm.

KEY

—— **Number of people in the Superdome**

—— **Number of National Guard Troops in New Orleans**

Food and drinkable water are in short supply in New Orleans. More than 20,000 people are sheltered in the Superdome. Police try to stop looting in the city. Mayor Nagin calls for a total evacuation. Governor Blanco and staff search for buses to evacuate people from the city. The Coast Guard has rescued 1,250 people. Greatly diminished in power, Katrina becomes part of a frontal zone over the Great Lakes.

Wednesday, August 31

Governor Blanco estimates death toll in the thousands (the actual toll is much lower) and requests 40,000 troops. National Guard troops assist in the evacuation of the Superdome. The Coast Guard has rescued twenty-nine hundred people.

Thursday, September 1

Military vehicles bring food and supplies. Fifteen hundred people remain in the Superdome. Governor Blanco and Mayor Nagin meet with President Bush, who proposes that he assume control of National Guard forces in the area. The National Guard secures the convention center. The Coast Guard has rescued 4,000 people.

Friday, September 2

20,000	**20,000**	**1,500**
4,700	**7,400**	**8,600**

HURRICANE KATRINA TIMELINE

Hurricane Katrina is upgraded to a category 5 storm, with wind speeds up to 175 mph. Mayor Nagin orders a mandatory evacuation and opens ten "refuges of last resort." Lines form at the New Orleans Superdome as 10,000 people unable to evacuate the city seek shelter.

Sunday, August 28

10,000
3,500

Hurricane Katrina makes landfall near Buras, Louisiana, as a category 3 storm, with wind speeds of up to 120 mph. Governor Blanco urges evacuees to stay out of New Orleans. New Orleans city police begin search and rescue operations in heavily flooded areas. The Coast Guard begins rescue operations, airlifting stranded victims from rooftops. The first levee breaches are reported.

Monday, August 29

10,000
3,500

Most of New Orleans is underwater, and there is widespread looting of homes and stores. Twelve thousand people are now sheltering at the Superdome. Seventy-five hundred National Guard troops are called up in Louisiana, Mississippi, and Alabama. Governor Blanco requests evacuation of the Superdome. The Coast Guard has rescued more than 1,000 people. The hurricane continues to move northeastward, weakening over land, and is downgraded to a tropical depression over the Tennessee valley.

Tuesday, August 30

12,000
3,800

Evacuations speed up. Governor Blanco rejects the White House proposal and hires James Lee Witt, a former FEMA director, to manage National Guard forces. The Guard has evacuated tens of thousands of people from the city by land and air.

Saturday, September 3

12,000

Troops patrol the streets and regain control of the city. The National Guard assists police officers as they begin to urge holdouts to leave the city.

Sunday, September 4

12,000

Two levees are fixed. With looting and violence subsiding, National Guard officials declare New Orleans secure. The Coast Guard says it has rescued more than 18,000 people from flooded areas of New Orleans.

Monday, September 5

16,000

SOURCE NOTES

Where I grew up, hurricanes are as much a part of life as the flow of the seasons. If it's summertime in south Florida, it must be time to check the storm shutters.

Years after the hurricanes of my childhood, I began covering hurricanes as a newspaper reporter. Mostly, it happened by chance. There would be a hurricane and I would be where the storm was heading. Or I would be in New York and an editor would send me.

Then I started getting more interested in hurricanes and volunteering for hurricane duty. I began thinking about writing a book about hurricanes. After my coverage of Hurricane Katrina, Alex Ward, the editor of the *New York Times* book department, asked me to write this book.

The core of the book came from my experiences with hurricanes over many years, as well as feelings and ideas I picked up along the way—from the afternoon I drove home early from a summer job to help my family board up our house in Hollywood, Florida, to the days of wading through gunky water in New Orleans in 2005, when I should have been old enough to know better.

Of course a big part of my hurricane experience has been the hundreds of conversations with people before, during, and after storms; people who were making preparations, people who were evacuating, people who lost everything, people who lost nothing, people who were rescued, people who were rescuing others. There are endless small scenes in my memory, like the night right after Hurricane Wilma when I stood outside under a generator-powered light in the little town of South Bay, Florida, as members of the city council, firemen, and neighbors worked at tables, ladling out stew and mashed potatoes to migrant workers whose mobile homes had been wrecked.

Experts who have spent their lives tracking hurricanes and thinking about how they work helped me understand these creatures. And for many foundation facts, I turned to the treasury of data provided on the Internet Web sites of the National Hurricane Center and its parent, the National Oceanic and Atmospheric Administration (see "Internet Resources" for URLs).

Woven into this book are ideas, images, and facts gathered from scientific articles, newspaper and magazine reports, and books on weather and hurricanes.

Of all the books I read, the most helpful (and the one I will be taking with me as I cover future hurricanes) is *Hurricane Watch,* by Bob Sheets, a former director of the National Hurricane Center, and Jack Williams, the founding editor of the *USA Today* Weather Page. *Hurricane Watch* helped me quickly get a sweeping sense of the subject of hurricanes and was very good on scientific and historical detail. The anecdote in Chapter 3 of this book about Grady Norton, the first head of the National Hurricane Center, and how he often sought guidance for his forecasts through prayer, came from *Hurricane Watch.*

Divine Wind, by Kerry Emanuel, an atmospheric scientist at M.I.T., was also helpful on the science of hurricanes and historic highlights, including details on the pilots and crews that fly into storms and take their pulse.

The Hurricane and Its Impact, by Robert H. Simpson, another former head of the National Hurricane Center, and Herbert Rieh; and *Atlantic Hurricanes,* by Gordon E. Dunn, also a former director of the National Hurricane Center, and Banner I. Miller, a colleague at the National Hurricane Center, were comprehensive and filled with insights. Pete Davies' *Inside the Hurricane* and Jay Barnes' *Florida's Hurricane History* were also very helpful.

In some brief and clearly written passages, Ernest Zebrowski Jr., in *Perils of a Restless Planet,* helped me understand how hurricanes are born.

Joseph Conrad in *Typhoon* and Jack London in some of his short stories provided riveting depictions of the ferocity of hurricanes on people, ships, and coastal environs. In *Hurricane,* Marjory Stoneman Douglas, best known for her writing about the Everglades, added fresh ways of looking at the world's most destructive storms.

The Hurricane Handbook, by Sharon Maddux Carpenter and Toni Garcia Carpenter, is a compact guide that hits the high points of hurricanes and their journey through history. I also benefited from dipping into *Hurricanes, Their Nature and Impacts on Society,* by Roger A. Pielke Jr. and Roger A. Pielke Sr.

Many authors concentrated on a single hurricane and deepened my knowledge and intuitive sense of what hurricanes can do and how, over the years, hurricane forecasters and researchers have worked.

Isaac's Storm, by Erik Larson, is the story of one of the pioneers in the study of hurricanes, Isaac Monroe Cline, and the hurricane of 1900 that destroyed Galveston, Texas, killing perhaps 12,000 people, including Cline's wife. In *Through a Night of Horrors,* I read a collection of letters from survivors of the Galveston hurricane edited by Casey Edward Greene and Shelly Henley Kelly.

In *Black Cloud,* Eliot Kleinberg wrote about the great Florida hurricane of 1928 that killed more than 1,800 people around Lake Okeechobee. Robert Mykle gave his rendition of the storm in *Killer 'Cane.*

Willie Drye wrote about the Labor Day hurricane in the Florida Keys in 1935 in *Storm of the Century.* Phil Scott called his book about the 1935 storm *Hemingway's Hurricane.* The writer Ernest Hemingway, who lived in Key West among other places, drew attention to the disaster with articles that blamed the federal government for the deaths of hundreds of destitute World War I veterans who had been hired build a highway running through the Keys.

Two books on the 1938 hurricane that mauled Long Island, New York, and the coasts of New England were helpful. One of them, *Sudden Storm,* was written by R. A. Scott. The other, *The Great Hurricane: 1938,* was written by Cherie Burns.

SOURCE NOTES

Philip D. Hearn, a former reporter for United Press International, wrote a detailed account of the 1969 hurricane that had defined disaster along the Mississippi coast until Katrina proved that even more wreckage was possible. He called his book *Hurricane Camille, Monster Storm of the Gulf Coast.*

Marq de Villiers produced a readable and useful book of great breadth in *Windswept: The Story of Wind and Weather.*

Historical hurricane information used to create the map on page 106 came from the National Oceanographic and Atmospheric Administration Web site (www.noaa.gov).

The following articles from the archives of *The New York Times* were adapted for use as textboxes and supplemental material:

Ch. 1: New Orleans, 2005

Pg. 10: "Different Names for the Storms." *The New York Times*, May 4, 1991.

Pg. 14: Carter, Bill. "Modest Storm Was a Major TV Event." *The New York Times*, July 15, 1996.

Ch. 2: The Storm Factory

Pg. 18: Revkin, Andrew C. "Now They Even Have Names: Currents That Turn Storms into Monsters." *The New York Times*, September 27, 2005.

Pg. 26: Broad, William J. "A Weather Change Worth Celebrating." *The New York Times*, March 21, 2000.

Ch. 3: Hurricane Hunting

Pg. 32: Leary, Warren E. "Flurry of Satellites to Monitor Earth and Examine Galaxy." *The New York Times*, December 10, 2002.

Pg. 36: Browne, Malcolm. "Daring Hurricane Hunters Ride Rollercoaster in the Sky." *The New York Times*, September 18, 1988.

Ch. 4: Defining the Danger

Pg. 44: Revkin, Andrew C. "After Pinpointing Tracking, Forecasting Turns to Intensity." *The New York Times*, September 18, 2003.

Pg. 49: Revkin, Andrew C. "Global Warming Is Expected to Raise Hurricane Intensity." *The New York Times*, September 30, 2004.

Ch. 5: Battening Down the Hatches

Pg. 57: Dean, Cornelia, and Andrew C. Revkin. "After Centuries of 'Controlling' Land, Gulf Residents Learn Who's Really the Boss." *The New York Times*, August 30, 2005.

Pg. 59: Oshinsky, David. "Hell and High Water." *The New York Times*, July 9, 2006.

Ch. 6: Into the Strike Zone

Pg. 72: Dewan, Shaila, and Janet Roberts. "Louisiana's Deadly Storm Took Strong as Well as the Helpless." *The New York Times*, December 18, 2005.

Pg. 76: Dwyer, Jim, and Christopher Drew. "Fear Exceeded Crime's Reality in New Orleans." *The New York Times*, September 29, 2005.

Ch. 7: Riding It Out

Pg. 82: Revkin, Andrew C. "But Where Is It Going?" *The New York Times*, September 14, 2004.

Pg. 84: Stevens, William K. "Panic Stations: The Fine Art of Hurricane Hype." *The New York Times*, October 4, 1998.

Ch. 8: Shelter from the Storm

Pg. 86: Jenkins, Lee. "Superdome Stars: Everyday People Confronted Chaos." *The New York Times*, August 6, 2006.

Pg. 95: Lyman, Rick. "Among Elderly Evacuees, a Strong Desire to Return Home, but Nowhere to Go," *The New York Times*, July 24, 2006.

Ch. 9: Bracing for the Future

Pg. 96: Dean, Cornelia. "Some Experts Say Its Time to Evacuate the Coast (for Good)." *The New York Times*, October 4, 2005

Pg. 102: Alford, Jeremy. "After Hard Lessons, a New Game Plan for Hurricane Seasons." *The New York Times*, March 29, 2006.

Building a Hurricane-Proof House

Pg. 104: Treaster, Joseph B. "Let a Hurricane Huff and Puff: Coastal Builders Are Finding Eager Buyers for Fortified Houses." *The New York Times*, June 22, 2006.

Hurricane Katrina Timeline

Pg. 108: Drew, Christopher, Eric Lipton, David Rohde, and Scott Shane. "Storm and Crisis: Government Assistance." *The New York Times*, September 11, 2005.

FURTHER READING

If you are interested in learning more about some of the subjects covered in this book, you may enjoy reading the following articles from *The New York Times*:

Africa and hurricane formation
Stevens, William K. "More Strong Hurricanes Predicted for East in Next 2 Decades." *The New York Times*, September 25, 1990.

Building standards
Applebome, Peter. "After the Storm: A New Look at Construction Standards." *The New York Times*, September 6, 1992.
Quint, Michael. "A Storm Over Housing Codes." *The New York Times*, December 1, 1995.

Coastal development
Applebome, Peter. "Storm Cycles and Coastal Development Could Make Disaster a Way of Life." *The New York Times*, August 30, 1992.
Dean, Cornelia. "Dauphin Island Shows How a Hurricane Shifts Natural Processes into Fast Forward." *The New York Times*, September 20, 2005.
Revkin, Andrew C. "Climate Experts Warn of More Coastal Building." *The New York Times*, July 25, 2006.

Forecasting
Broad, William J. "Storm Forecast Seen as Primitive Art." *The New York Times*, September 27, 1985.
"Scientists Looking to Improve Measure of Storm Dangers." *The New York Times*, November 27, 1998.
"In West Africa, a Storm Is Born." *The New York Times*, November 9, 1998.
Olson, Elizabeth. "Unnatural Weather, Natural Disasters: A New U.N. Focus." *The New York Times*, May 18, 2004.

Great Hurricane of 1900
"Great Disaster at Galveston." *The New York Times*, September 10, 1900.
"Many Towns Wrecked: Mass Destruction and Great Loss of Life in the Path of the Storm Inland." *The New York Times*, September 10, 1900.

"The Wrecking of Galveston: Story Told in Detail by Newspaper Man Who Escaped." *The New York Times*, September 11, 1900.

"The Storm-Swept City." *The New York Times*, September 11, 1900.

Hurricane hunters

"Army Airmen Fly to Storm's Center." *The New York Times*, September 15, 1945.

"40 on Plane Ride Storm." *The New York Times*, October 13, 1947.

Thorne, B. K. "U.S. Fliers Plot Hurricane's Course by Riding Right into Storm Clouds." *The New York Times*, August 31, 1951.

"'Hunters' Picture Hurricane Wrath." *The New York Times*, September 12, 1954.

Brown, Nona B. "Flying into the Hurricane's Eye." *The New York Times*, August 21, 1955.

King, Wayne. "Flights in Eye Give Best Data on Hurricanes." *The New York Times*, September 2, 1979.

Hurricane Andrew (1992)

Barron, James. "Hurricane Rips Through Florida and Heads into Gulf." *The New York Times*, August 18, 1992.

Stevens, William K. "Hurricane Surprised Forecasters." *The New York Times*, August 26, 1992.

Applebome, Peter. "In the Hurricane Belt, a New, Wary Respect." *The New York Times*, August 18, 1993.

Hurricane Camille (1969)

Associated Press. "Hurricane Stuns Mississippi Coast as 200,000 Flee." *The New York Times*, August 18, 1969.

Reed, Roy. "What the Hurricane Did." *The New York Times*, August 19, 1969.

Associated Press. "Hurricane Dead Reported at 101." *The New York Times*, August 19, 1969.

Associated Press. "Limited Martial Law Set by Mississippi Governor." *The New York Times*, August 20, 1969.

Hurricane Katrina, events surrounding

Treaster, Joseph B., and Abby Goodnough. "Powerful Storm Threatens Havoc Along Gulf Coast." *The New York Times*, August 29, 2005.

Treaster, Joseph B. , and Kate Zernike. "Hurricane Slams into Gulf Coast. Dozens Are Dead." *The New York Times*, August 30, 2005.

Treaster, Joseph B., and N. R. Kleinfield. "New Orleans Is Inundated as Two Levees Fail." *The New York Times*, August 31, 2005.

McFadden, Robert D., and Ralph Blumenthal. "Bush Sees Long Recovery for New Orleans: 30,000 Troops in Largest U.S. Relief Effort." *The New York Times*, September 1, 2005.

Treaster, Joseph B., and Deborah Sontag. "Despair and Lawlessness Grip New Orleans as Thousands Remain Stranded in Squalor." *The New York Times*, September 2, 2005.

Berenson, Alex, and Sewell Chan. "Forced Evacuation of a Battered New Orleans Begins." *The New York Times*, September 9, 2005.

Shane, Scott, and Thom Shanker. "The Response: When Storm Hit, National Guard Was Deluged, Too." *The New York Times*, September 28, 2005.

Schwartz, John. "An Autopsy of Katrina: Four Storms, Not Just One." *The New York Times*, May 30, 2006.

Hurricane Mitch (1998)

"Hurricane Hits Coasts of Honduras and Belize." *The New York Times*, October 28, 1998.

Rohter, Larry. "Flood Toll Estimate Rises Above 1,000 in Central America." *The New York Times*, November 2, 1998.

McKinley, James C., Jr., "Hondurans Sift a Storm's Debris." *The New York Times*, November 5, 1998.

Hurricane Rita (2005)

Williams, Timothy, and Cornelia Dean. "Wary and Weary, Gulf Eyes a New Storm." *The New York Times*, September 20, 2005.

Yardley, William, and Abby Goodnough. " Residents Leave Gulf Coast Area as Storm Grows." *The New York Times*, September 21, 2005.

Romero, Simon. "Gulf Storm of Top Strength Menaces Texas." *The New York Times*, September 22, 2005.

Blumenthal, Ralph. "Miles of Traffic as Texans Heed Order to Leave." *The New York Times*, September 23, 2005.

Lyman, Rick, and Laura Griffin. "Traffic Deaths: Bus Evacuating Seniors Burns, Killing 24 Near Dallas." *The New York Times*, September 23, 2005.

Blumenthal, Ralph, and David Barstow. "'Katrina Effect' Pushed Texans into Gridlock." *The New York Times*, September 24, 2005.

Labor Day Hurricane of 1935

Associated Press. "Both Coasts Threatened: Miami, Palm Beach and

Sarasota Menaced by Tropical Storm." *The New York Times,* September 3, 1935.

Associated Press. "Hurricane's Toll 100" *The New York Times*, September 4, 1935.

Associated Press. "Veterans' Camp Wrecked by Storm." *The New York Times*, September 4, 1935.

Lewis, Spearman. "Air Survey Shows Havoc in the Keys." *The New York Times*, September 5, 1935.

Naming system

White, Peter T. "Why Gales Are Gals." *The New York Times*, September 26, 1954.

New England and hurricanes

Stevens, William K. "Historic Hurricane Could Catch Northeast with Its Guard Down." *The New York Times*, August 23, 1994.

Revkin, Andrew C. "Experts Unearth a Stormy Past." *The New York Times*, July 24, 2001.

Rather, John. "Dreading a Replay of the 1938 Hurricane." *The New York Times*, August 28, 2005.

Barron, James. "Evaluating a What-If Case: New York's Evacuation." *The New York Times*, September 24, 2005.

New England Hurricane of 1938

"Hurricane Veering from Florida: May Keep Its Course Out to Sea." *The New York Times*, September 20, 1938.

"Storm's Full Fury Hits Long Island." *The New York Times*, September 22, 1938.

"Cape Cod Isolated: 20 Believed Dead." *The New York Times*, September 23, 1938.

McCaffrey, James P. "Hurricane Victims Swept into Sea as Tidal Wave Hit Rhode Island." *The New York Times*, September 23, 1938.

"Night of Terror Told by Countess." *The New York Times*, September 23, 1938.

Rather, John. "'38 Hurricane Still a Lesson in Ruin." *The New York Times*, June 13, 1999.

Clavin, Tom. "Blown Away." *The New York Times*, September 14, 2003.

New Orleans, evacuees

Lyman, Rick, and Susan Saulny. "Shelters: Still Sheltered, Evacuees Take a Longer View." *The New York Times*, September 22, 2005.

Yardley, William. "The Convention Center: Where Disorder Once Reigned, Efficient Evacuation Now Rules." *The New York Times*, September 22, 2005.

Dewan, Shaila. "Evacuee Study Finds Declining Health." *The New York Times*, April 18, 2006.

New Orleans, readiness for future storms

"New Orleans's Hurricane Problem." *The New York Times*, July 4, 2003.

Marsh, Bill. "Ideas and Trends: What Will It Take to Safeguard New Orleans?" *The New York Times*, September 11, 2005.

Broad, William. "High-Tech Flood Control with Nature's Help." *The New York Times*, September 6, 2005.

Drew, Christopher, and Andrew C. Revkin. "The Defenses: Design Flaws Seen in New Orleans Flood Walls." *The New York Times*, September 21, 2005.

Alford, Jeremy. "After Hard Lessons, a New Game Plan for Hurricane Seasons." *The New York Times*, March 29, 2006.

Alford, Jeremy. "New Orleans Preps for the Storm Next Time." *The New York Times*, May 24, 2006.

Schwartz, John. "Levees Rebuilt Just in Time, but Doubts Remain." *The New York Times*, May 25, 2006.

Associated Press. "New Orleans' Preparedness Still at Issue." *The New York Times*, August 28, 2006.

New Orleans, rebuilding

Rivlin, Gary. "New Orleans Commission to Seek Overhaul of Schools and Transit." *The New York Times*, January 11, 2006.

Nossiter, Adam. "In New Orleans, Money Is Ready but a Plan Isn't." *The New York Times*, June 18, 2006.

Eaton, Leslie. "Hurricane Aid Finally Flowing to Homeowners." *The New York Times*, July 17, 2006.

Saulny, Susan. "Despite a City's Hopes, an Uneven Population." *The New York Times*, July 30, 2006.

Nossiter, Adam. "Outlines Emerge for a Shaken New Orleans." *The New York Times*, August 27, 2006.

Nossiter, Adam. "Two Visions for New Orleans, One of Plenty, One of Ruin."

The New York Times, August 27, 2006.

Readiness, individual

Warde, John. "Home Clinic: Batten Down the Hatches, Tie Down the Patio
    Set." *The New York Times*, July 5, 1992.

Romano, Jay. "Protecting Pets in a Disaster." *The New York Times*,
    September 25, 2005.

Readiness, national

Goodnough, Abby. "As Hurricane Season Looms, States Aim to Scare." *The
    New York Times*, May 31, 2006.

Lipton, Eric. "U.S. Report Faults Nation's Preparedness for Disaster." *The
    New York Times*, June 17, 2006.

Satellites

Finney, John W. "Satellite to Act as Hurricane Spy." *The New York Times*,
    May 29, 1961.

Chang, Kenneth. "Officials Report Progress in Weather Satellite Effort."
    The New York Times, June 9, 2006.

Storm control attempts

Kaempffert, Waldemar. "Making Weather to Order." *The New York Times*,
    July 40, 1947.

"Plane Scans Storm for 'Busting' Test." *The New York Times*, September 9, 1947.

Porter, Russell. "Cloud-Seeding Fails as a Storm Control." *The New York
    Times*, April 16, 1955.

Shuster, Alvin. "Rain-Making Test Planned by U.S." *The New York Times*,
    May 2, 1955.

Kimble, George H. T. "Storm Clouds Over Weather Control." *The New York
    Times*, February 9, 1958.

INTERNET RESOURCES

Many government agencies, news organizations, clubs, and individuals maintain Web sites with hurricane information. The following sites are a good starting place for further research:

The National Oceanographic and Atmospheric Administration (NOAA) can be found at www.noaa.gov.

The National Hurricane Center, a division of NOAA, maintains a homepage at www.nhc.noaa.gov. It includes an information page on how to plan for a hurricane and a timeline of historical storms.

The Climate Prediction Center, which forecasts the severity of upcoming hurricane seasons, is located online at www.cpc.ncep.noaa.gov.

The National Weather Service is at National Oceanographic and Atmospheric Administration, at www.nws.noaa.gov.

You can find information about the history and future of hurricane research at the homepage of the Hurricane Research Division of the Atlantic Oceanographic and Meteorological Laboratory, www.aoml.noaa.gov/hrd.

The 53rd Weather Reconnaissance Squadron (also known as the hurricane hunters) maintains a Web site with pictures, FAQs, and stories at www.hurricanehunters.com.

The Federal Emergency Management Agency's (FEMA)'s site for kids is at www.fema.gov/kids.

Acknowledgments

Many people contributed to the making of this book. Special thanks to Larry Ingrassia and Alex Ward of *The New York Times.* Deirdre Langeland was a creative and visionary editor. Robert H. Simpson, a former director of the National Hurricane Center, Hugh Willoughby, a professor at Florida International University and former director of the Hurricane Research Division of the National Oceanographic and Atmospheric Administration, and Andrew Revkin, a science writer and colleague at *The Times,* were particularly generous with their time.

Thanks also to Terry Aguayo, Ron Alleyne, Donna Anderson, Gloria Anderson, Stephen R. Baig, Gloria Bell, Maggie Berkvist, George K. Bernstein, Don Bohning, Gerry Bohning, Daniel P. Brown, Dana Canedy, Hugh D. Cobb III, Nicholas K. Coch, Charles Competello, Alain Delaqueriere, Philippe Diederich, Barbara Dill, Christopher Drew, Susan England, Bernadette Espina, Joy Fortune, James L. Franklin, Marko Georgiev, Abby Goodnough, Jerry M. Gray, Amy Halsey, Douglas M. Halsey, Heather Hanley, Robert P. Hartwig, James Horwitz, J. Robert Hunter, Sandra Jameson, David Cay Johnston, Philip J. Klotzbach, Richard Knabb, Robert Korose, Howard Kunruther, Chris Landsea, Chang Lee, Sheriff Ronnie Lee, Frank Lepore, John Thomas Longo, Max Mayfield, Gaynell C. Methvin, Ken Meyn, Alison N. Mitchell, Marva Mitchell, Tomi Murata, Stuart Newman, Adam Nossiter, Tim O'Hara, Barbara Oliver, Richard J. Pasch, Edward Pasterick, John Pavone, Alexandra Pelletier, Ed Rappaport, Steve Rautenberg, Alison Rea, Capt. Don Rodriguez, Pedro Rosado, John Schwartz, Peggy Simpson, Steve Smith, David Snyder, Stacey Stewart, Leonard Ray Teel, the Treaster Family, Robert Trinka, Gilbert White, Carolyn Wilder, Marvin Wolf, and Loretta Worters.

PICTURE CREDITS

The publisher would like to thank the following for permission to reproduce their material. Every care has been taken to trace copyright holders. However, if there have been unintentional omissions or failure to trace copyright holders, we apologize and will, if informed, endeavor to make corrections in any future edition.

Front Cover: (main) Jose Luis Pelaez, Inc./Corbis; (overlay) Daniel Smith/zefa/Corbis; Back Cover: (left) Mike Theiss/Jim Reed Photography/Corbis; (right) Alan Schein Photography/Corbis

Page 1: Tracy Gitnik/AP Images/Empics; 2–3: Scott Dommin/Hurricane Hunters; 4–5: Mike Theiss/Jim Reed Photography/Corbis; 6: Bill Haber/AP Images/Empics; 8: Chris Graythen/Getty Images; 11: Mark Wilson/Getty Images; 12–13: Ray Fairall/AP Images/Empics; 15: Charles W. Luzier/Reuters/Corbis; 16: NASA/Corbis; 17: NOAA; 19: NOAA; 20: AP Images/Empics; 21: NOAA; 22: *The New York Times* Archives; 23: Bettmann/Corbis; 24: *The New York Times*; 25: NOAA; 26: Kevin Fleming/Corbis; 27: NASA/GOES; 28: Scott Dommin/Hurricane Hunters; 28: NOAA; 30: Barbara Hernandez for *The New York Times*; 31: Joe Raedle/Getty Images; 33: Unisys Corp.; 34: Jim Sugar/Corbis; 35: NOAA; 37: Scott Dommin/Hurricane Hunters; 38: NOAA; 39: Gene Blevins/*LA Daily News*/Corbis; 40: NASA; 42: Andy Newman/AP Images/Empics; 43: NOAA; 46: Mike Theiss/Jim Reed Photography/Corbis; 47: NOAA; 50–51: Marc Serota/Reuters/Corbis; 51: Lynne Sladky/AP Images/Empics; 52: Richard Cummins/Corbis; 53: Andy Newman/AP Images/Empics; 54: Paul Buck/epa/Corbis; 55: Joe Skipper/Reuters/Corbis; 56: Rick Wilking/Reuters/Corbis; 59: NOAA; 60: Cheryl Gerber/AP Images/Empics; 61: Michael Ainsworth/Dallas Morning News/Corbis; 62: Paul Buck/epa/Corbis; 63: Alan Diaz/AP Images/Empics; 64: Dave Martin/AP Images/Empics; 65: Mark Wilson/Getty Images; 66: Warren Faidley/Corbis; 67: Marianne Todd/Getty Images; 68: Rick Wilking/Reuters/Corbis; 70: Dave Martin/AP Images/Empics; 71: NASA; 73: Kyle Niemie/US Coast Guard; 74: Douglas Clifford/St. Petersburg Times; 75: Marko Georgiev for *The New York Times*; 77: NASA; 78: Dave Martin/AP Images/Empics; 80: Bryan Snyder/Getty Images; 81: Scott Martin/AP Images/Empics; 82: NASA; 83: Stan Honda/AFP/Getty Images; 85: Vincent LaForet/*The New York Times*; 86: Michael Ainsworth/*Dallas Morning News*/Corbis; 87: Brett Coomer/*Houston Chronicle*/AP; 88: Kelly Owen/ZUMA/Corbis; 89: Eric Gay/AP Images/Empics; 90: Marko Georgiev for *The New York Times*; 91: Chris O'Meara/AP Images/Empics; 92: Gary Coronado/Palm Beach Post; 93: Rick Wilking/Reuters/Corbis; 94: Gary I Rothstein/Reuters/Corbis; 96: Spencer Platt/Getty Images; 99: Jose Fuste Raga/Corbis; 101: Phil Coale/AP Images/Empics; 103: Joe Raedle/Getty Images; 105: *New York Times* Graphics; 106–7: Nik Keevil; 108–9 (background): Nicholas Kamm/AFP/Getty Images.

INDEX